Harvard Business Review

ON

SALES AND SELLING

D0061695

3/11

THE HARVARD BUSINESS REVIEW PAPERBACK SERIES

The series is designed to bring today's managers and professionals the fundamental information they need to stay competitive in a fast-moving world. From the preeminent thinkers whose work has defined an entire field to the rising stars who will redefine the way we think about business, here are the leading minds and landmark ideas that have established the *Harvard Business Review* as required reading for ambitious businesspeople in organizations around the globe.

Other books in the series:

Harvard Business Review Interviews with CEOs

Harvard Business Review on Advances in Strategy

Harvard Business Review on Appraising Employee Performance

Harvard Business Review on Becoming a High Performance Manager

Harvard Business Review on Brand Management

Harvard Business Review on Breakthrough Leadership

Harvard Business Review on Breakthrough Thinking

Harvard Business Review on Bringing Your Whole Self to Work

Harvard Business Review on Building Personal and Organizational Resilience

Harvard Business Review on the Business Value of IT

Harvard Business Review on Change

Harvard Business Review on Compensation

Harvard Business Review on Corporate Ethics

Harvard Business Review on Corporate Governance

Harvard Business Review on Corporate Responsibility

Harvard Business Review on Corporate Strategy

Harvard Business Review on Crisis Management

Harvard Business Review on Culture and Change

Harvard Business Review on Customer Relationship Management

Other books in the series (continued):

Harvard Business Review

ON

SALES AND SELLING

The Harvard Business Review articles in this collection are available as
individual reprints. Discounts apply to quantity purchases. For information and ordering, please contact Customer Service, Harvard Business
School Publishing, Boston, MA 02163. Telephone: (617) 783-7500 or
(800) 988-0886, 8 A.M. to 6 P.M. Eastern Time, Monday through Friday.
Fax: (617) 783-7555, 24 hours a day. E-mail: custserv@hbsp.harvard.edu.

Library of Congress cataloging information forthcoming
ISBN 978-1-4221-4591-3

Contents

The New Science of Sales Force Productivity   1
DIANNE LEDINGHAM, MARK KOVAC, AND HEIDI LOCKE SIMON

How to Pitch a Brilliant Idea   23
KIMBERLY D. ELSBACH

What Makes a Good Salesman   41
DAVID MAYER AND HERBERT M. GREENBERG

Low-Pressure Selling   63
EDWARD C. BURSK

Making the Major Sale   97
BENSON P. SHAPIRO AND RONALD S. POSNER

Major Sales:
Who Really Does the Buying?   123
THOMAS V. BONOMA

Humanize Your Selling Strategy   149
HARVEY B. MACKAY

Manage the Customer, Not Just the Sales Force   167
BENSON P. SHAPIRO

About the Contributors   189

Index   191

The New Science of
Sales Force Productivity

DIANNE LEDINGHAM, MARK KOVAC, AND
HEIDI LOCKE SIMON

Executive Summary

FOR YEARS, sales managers at many companies have
relied on top performers and sheer numbers of sales reps
to stay competitive. But while they may have squeaked
by on this wing-and-a-prayer technique, their sales teams
haven't thrived the way they once did.

Today's most successful sales leaders are taking a
more scientific approach. Savvy managers are reshap-
ing their tactics in response to changing markets. They
are reaching out to new customers in innovative ways.
And they are increasing productivity by helping the reps
they already have make the most of their skills and
resources.

Leaders who take a scientific approach to sales force
effectiveness have learned to use four levers to boost
their reps' productivity in a predictable and manageable

1

way. First, they systematically target their firms' offerings, matching the right products with the right customers. Second, they optimize the automation, tools, and procedures at their disposal, providing reps with the support they need to boost sales. Third, they analyze and manage their reps' performance, measuring both internal processes and results to determine where their teams' strengths and weaknesses are. Fourth, they pay close attention to sales force deployment—how well sales, support, marketing, and delivery resources are matched to customers.

These four levers can help sales leaders increase productivity across the board, the authors say, though they have the greatest impact on lower-ranked performers. The overall effect of increasing the average sales per employee can be exponential; it means a company won't have to rely on just a few talented individuals to stay competitive. This is especially important because finding and keeping star salespeople is more difficult than ever. What's more, managers who optimize the sales forces they already have can see returns they never thought possible.

Bob brody leaned back in his chair, frowning. Corporate wanted another 8% increase in sales from his division this year, and guess whose shoulders that goal would fall on? Ah, for the good old days, when he could just announce a 10% target, spread it like peanut butter over all his territories, then count on the sales reps for each region or product line to deliver. Sure, some would fall short, but the real rainmakers would make up the difference. Today, the purchasing departments of Bob's customers used algorithms to choose vendors for routine buys; pure economics often trumped personal relationships. For more complex sales, purchasing wanted customized end-to-end solutions. There's no way one person could close those deals, no matter how much golf he or she played. Most of the time, you needed a team of product and industry experts, not to mention rich incentives and a lot of back-office support.

The fact was—he knew he'd have to face it sooner or later—Bob was overwhelmed. Nothing about the sales process was as simple or predictable as it used to be. Eight percent growth? He wasn't even sure where to start.

IF THIS LITTLE FABLE sounds familiar, it's because managers often face similar problems. Over the past few years, we have worked through these sorts of challenges with dozens of senior executives in Brody's position. Even though the world around them was changing, they were still handing down targets from higher management and religiously putting more feet on the street, hoping that some of those new reps would once again save the day. Even arbiters of best practice such as General Electric can recall the wing-and-a-prayer style that, until recently, characterized their sales efforts. The company would give each individual his or her patch and say, "Good luck, and go get 'em," observes GE's Michael Pilot, who started his career 22 years ago as a salesperson at the organization and is now president of U.S. Equipment Financing, a unit of GE Commercial Finance.

Today, the savviest sales leaders are dramatically changing the way they run their groups. They are reinventing their sales approaches to respond to new market environments. They are expanding their lists of target customers beyond what anyone had previously considered. They are boosting their sales reps' productivity not by hiring the most-gifted individuals but by helping existing reps sell more. (See the exhibit "More Reps, or More Productivity?") As a result, their companies are growing at sometimes startling rates. Pilot's division—a large group in a mature industry—added $300 million in new business (about 10% organic growth) in 2005 alone, an improvement he attributes specifically to a reinvention of the operation's sales process. Similarly, SAP Americas, under president and CEO Bill McDermott, has more than doubled its software license business in three years, increasing its market share by 17 points.

What these leaders have in common might be called a scientific approach to sales force effectiveness. It's a method that puts systems around the art of selling, relying not just on gut feel and native sales talent—the traditional qualities of the rainmaker—but also on data, analysis, processes, and tools to redraw the boundaries of markets and increase a sales force's productivity. The goal isn't to replace rainmakers but to narrow the gap between the top 15% or 20% and the rest of the sales force. Companies that use the tactic well have found that, while even top sellers do better, reps in the lower quartiles show dramatic improvement, with productivity jumps of 200%. Such increases enhance the performance of the sales team as a whole and enable a company to reduce the expense of hiring new reps. Some firms using the approach have seen their average sales per rep increase by as much as 50% in two or three years, though most gains cluster around the 30% mark.

No latter-day Arthur Miller is likely to write a play about the practitioners of the new method; the drama is in the results, not the details. But if "the future of business is to do things by design, not by chance," as one sales leader put it, this new science may be what's required of the men and women charged with bringing in a company's revenue.

Putting Science into Sales

GE's Pilot understands how extensive a reinvention can be. As recently as the mid-1990s, the company was still expecting sales teams to assemble and prioritize their own database of prospects for their territories. The company's field sales managers even manually classified all the names in the division's database as either high priority or low priority. "We relied on telephone books," recalls Pilot. "And newspapers. And signs on trucks as they went by or signs on buildings." By 2004, says Pilot, he knew that GE Commercial Finance had to "put some science into it."

Pilot's first step was to revise the way he segmented customers—by using data that included records of past company transactions. The new database held information such as four-digit standard industrial classification codes, the type of equipment being leased, and so on. Then Pilot asked his field managers to create a list of prospective-customer characteristics, criteria that they believed would correlate with a customer's likelihood of doing business with GE. He took the 14 features they came up with, ran regression equations against the database of transactions, and identified six criteria that had high correlations. If a prospective customer tested well on those six criteria—such as predicted capital expenditures and number of filings for new business transactions—the probability that it would do business with GE was high.

More Reps, or More Productivity?

Companies that choose to take a scientific approach to sales force effectiveness may want to evaluate the two options shown here. The growth target for this fictitious global manufacturer—in this case an increase in revenues of $1.1 billion over five years—can be attained through various combinations of productivity improvements and new hires. But the cheapest and most effective route is usually to increase productivity as much as possible through use of the four levers—targeted offerings; optimized automation, tools, and procedures; performance management; and sales force deployment—and only then to put more feet on the street. The management challenge is ensuring that you have put enough science into your sales organization to drive that productivity predictably.

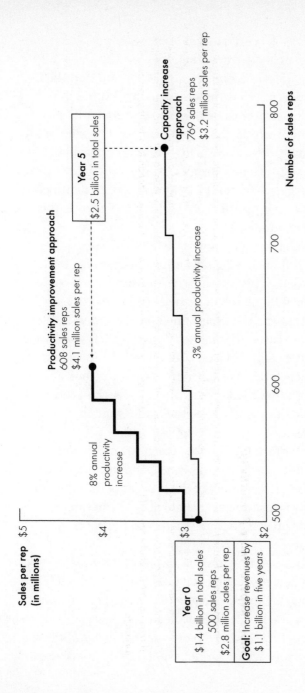

Sales per rep
(in millions)

$5

$4

$3

$2

Productivity improvement approach
608 sales reps
$4.1 million sales per rep

8% annual
productivity
increase

Year 5
$2.5 billion in total sales

Capacity increase approach
769 sales reps
$3.2 million sales per rep

3% annual productivity increase

Year 0
$1.4 billion in total sales
500 sales reps
$2.8 million sales per rep

Goal: Increase revenues by $1.1 billion in five years

500   600   700   800

Number of sales reps

The division scored its list of prospects based on the six attributes and then worked the new list for a while. Something interesting emerged. "We found that the top 30% of prospective customers were three times more likely to do a deal with us than the bottom 70%," says Pilot. In other words, that top group was made up of the new highest-priority prospects—and yet only about half of them had previously been classified as high priority by sales managers. The company had, in effect, identified 10,000 new high-priority prospects that it would otherwise have overlooked.

But it wasn't just the increase in sales acreage that made the difference; the new information also allowed Pilot to redesign his sales force. For example, he could take on the difficult job of restructuring territories, ensuring that each one contained plenty of opportunities. In some cases, that meant narrowing assigned areas based on the caliber of leads, reevaluating territories, or creating new territories entirely. "When you look at the market with that kind of scientific approach," Pilot says, "you'll never knowingly have territories that could intrinsically underdeliver."

On the performance management front, the data allowed Pilot to get new and less-experienced reps up to speed faster. "So much of the process of ramping up salespeople is just pointing them at the right targets," he says. "If you can do that, you'll get a big boost in productivity."

Pilot also used the information to support his sales force with new tools and processes for the field, such as targeted marketing campaigns that zeroed in on high-potential segments. Now every lead and piece of business generated gets tagged to a particular campaign. "It helps you think about what worked, what didn't, and where to double down and spend dollars for greater return on the marketing side," says Pilot.

The division's $300 million in new business for 2005 reflects both an increased sales pipeline and a 19% higher rate of conversion, or closings, in a market the company once believed was maturing. That revenue, Pilot notes, "is coming from customers that we know we wouldn't have been calling on" without the new approach. "At the end of the day," he says, "it's about building our business around customers and finding ways to help them grow."

Setting Targets

Setting annual sales objectives is any company's first step in creating a sales plan. Like our fictional Bob Brody, sales leaders have traditionally set goals based on upper management's aspirations for the company. Since those ambitions typically reflect shareholder expectations, they can't be ignored. But sales leaders too often apply the targets across every region and segment, without gathering the market and competitive data that would make their goals more realistic. Since variations across regions and segments are probable, sales reps often end up with quotas that are unrealistically high or low—either of which can demoralize and demotivate a sales force.

To see how the new science of goal setting works, consider how Cisco Systems uses technology to forecast sales. The company created a site where managers could log in and see up-to-the-minute sales performance— listed by region, product line, and so on—all the way down to the level of individual account executives. The site also contains data about reps' pipelines, including the size of each opportunity, what kind of technology the customer requires, and who the competitors are. Managers hold regular pipeline calls and produce new forecasts derived from the data every week. They then roll up the numbers into weekly, monthly, and quarterly forecasts. "The forecast accuracy for our quarterly numbers tends to be within plus or minus 1% to 2%," says Inder Sidhu, Cisco's vice president for worldwide sales strategy and planning.

Like other best-practice companies, Cisco isn't sitting still. Last year it provided its reps with state-of-the-art PDAs, and it's building custom applications for the devices designed to boost productivity. One such program speeds up data entry; another lets reps check their customers' recent activity (such as whether they have ordered parts or remitted an invoice). Cisco has also jump-started its reps' motivation by developing an online personal compensation rate calculator. "People can actually go in and say, 'OK, here's where I'm at right now in the quarter,' " says Sidhu. "It tells them exactly what the deal will mean to them [financially]."

Two years ago, Aggreko North America, a division of UK-based equipment rental company Aggreko, adopted a scientific approach to goal setting with dramatic results: In 2005, sales rose by 29%, and sales force productivity rose by 90%. Company president George Walker says that the process begins from the top down. Executives gather regional data on critical industry-level drivers in each of the company's vertical markets—oil refining, home construction, and so on—and then they calculate the firm's share of each market to set goals for growth. Next comes the bottom-up element: Armed with the data, area sales managers develop a view of territories, accounts, and quotas for individual reps by multiplying potential market size by target shares for each market. An iterative process between the local reps and senior management ensures that the expectations for individual salespeople are in line with overall corporate objectives.

Stepping Up Productivity

Traditionally, sales managers assumed that if you wanted to see significant growth, you had to look at last year's performance and then try to gauge how many new salespeople you could add, given the potential market and the ramp-up time that each new rep would require before generating revenue.

Companies that follow a scientific approach take a much different course. They focus above all on increasing individual salesperson productivity. They can do so because the question of how to boost productivity is no longer a mystery to them. (See the sidebar "TOPSales: A Science-Driven Approach" at the end of this article.) On the contrary, they have learned to use four levers that make productivity increases both predictable and manageable.

TARGETED OFFERINGS

Most organizations already know how to gather the data that enables them to segment their customer base. But companies pursuing a scientific approach boost productivity by taking segmentation one step further. They systematically divide their customers according to factors such as potential value of the account, share of wallet, vertical market, type of product, and type of sale. They define roles and align incentives to help sales reps position and sell the offerings that are most appropriate to each customer segment. Sales reps at these companies must have a deep understanding of the segments they serve: No one package of products and services fits all. And because many sales today can't be closed by just one individual, these companies know how to support a team approach with a careful architecture and smart management.

Targeted offerings aimed at individuals with a net worth of more than $25 million have made a big difference to Citigroup's private banking operation. That group serves business owners, real estate developers, lawyers, professional athletes, and other specialized segments, each with particular challenges and needs. "The industry has changed a lot in 15 years," says Todd Thomson, chairman and CEO of Citigroup's Global Wealth Management division. "It used to be about selling stocks and bonds and then mutual funds and other things. It was mostly transaction based." Today, Citigroup focuses less on selling investment products—commodities that can be bought and sold anywhere—and instead offers wealth management services and advice on how to reach short-, mid-, and long-term goals. The products, while still important, are secondary.

To make the transition, Citigroup stayed focused on two things. First, instead of simply growing its adviser and banker base, the firm made investments in the professional development of its people and platforms, such as by providing their private bankers with finance and business training taught by leading business school professors. Second, the company segmented its clients by type and created dedicated teams focused on supporting the needs of each client group. "We have a set of products, including risk management tools, that [have been crafted] and directed toward real estate developers," says Thomson. "When our private bankers and their teams show up to talk to a developer, we're smarter about what they need and how to deliver it than the competition is." The private bankers—the team coordinators—are encouraged to increase the reach of Citigroup's management expertise, which includes dealing with equities, fixed income, trust management, and even cash management for entrepreneurial businesses. "Over the past year, we've encouraged our people to think about how to solve [customers'] problems, and we've seen a massive increase in assets from those clients," Thomson says. The result: Citigroup's U.S. private bankers generate an average of $5.5 million per rep in revenue, compared with about $4 million average sales per rep in the rest of the industry.

OPTIMIZED AUTOMATION, TOOLS, AND PROCEDURES

"Sales force automation" has become a buzz term in recent years, and many companies are putting IT-based tools to work to improve sales force productivity. Aggreko North America uses CRM software with a "profitability predictor" that allows its reps to tweak an offering if margins aren't where they should be. GE Commercial Finance has Monday morning sales meetings that are facilitated by a "digital cockpit" that lets managers peer into reps' pipelines. Cisco, famed for its Web-based sales tools, knows that technology is effective only if it supplements and complements disciplined sales management processes (such as routine, detailed pipeline discussions based on a well-understood characterization of various stages in the pipeline and systematic channeling of leads to sales reps).

A dramatic transformation at SAP Americas, in particular, shows how important systematic processes can be. When McDermott took over in 2002, one of his first moves was to set standards for individual sales reps that reflected the market potential: $500,000 for the first quarter of the next year, $750,000 for the second quarter, and so on. The quarterly targets alone dramatically changed many people's thinking; traditionally, SAP reps had always counted on a big fourth quarter to pull themselves through the year. Instead of allowing reps to scramble to meet annual sales goals at the end of each year, McDermott set a pipeline standard. He expected reps to have three times their annual sales quotas in their pipeline of prospects on a rolling basis, quarter by quarter. To ensure that business partners (like IBM Global Services and Accenture, which implement the systems SAP sells) would be drawn into the selling effort, McDermott decided that at least half of each individual pipeline should be assigned to a business partner that would team up with SAP to close the deals.

Merely setting such goals, however, is not enough. Supporting them with management processes, selling materials, and automated tools for measuring leading indicators and results is what makes outcomes more predictable. For example, reps are regularly informed about key industry trends and about which of SAP's comprehensive product offerings will be most relevant and valuable that year for a target segment. When reps identify clients that could make better use of key SAP products to address an industry trend, "your whole marketing muscle and your pipeline muscle are really focused on letting those clients know that they're leaving hundreds of millions of dollars of value on the table," says McDermott.

PERFORMANCE MANAGEMENT

Most organizations have an expected level of sales attrition based on whether reps make their quotas over time. But some have added deeper levels of performance analysis that make sales productivity more predictable and thus more manageable. For instance, for each customer segment (such as global accounts, large-company accounts, and so on), SAP has analyzed how long it takes for new reps to become productive and how their productivity increases after that. They can also determine the average productivity rate for seasoned reps. This helps managers staff their segment territory plan more effectively. And it helps them know more quickly when a new hire isn't meeting the standard. "People generally reach their productivity plateau at 12 months," McDermott explains. "If they are not there, they are not going to get there. And that's about 10% of our new hires."

The key to retention is to set people up to succeed. That shouldn't be a matter of good fortune; it should be a result of data-driven planning. Every successful company we studied measures inputs—a rep's pipeline, time spent prospecting, or specific sales calls completed—as well as outputs, thereby helping the reps stay on top of the process. "If you're not looking at the in-process measures and you're simply looking at the results," says McDermott, "you're missing the most important element, which is the future."

The best companies offer development opportunities to successful reps. Thus Citigroup's Thomson, who also oversees the wealth management business of Smith Barney, a division of the company, notes that successful financial advisers at his firm not only keep a higher

percentage of the revenue they generate but also are
rewarded with professional development that enables
them to broaden and deepen their wealth management practices.

Data-driven companies also align incentives with the
behaviors that are critical to a rep's financial success.
That can entail adjusting metrics and commissions so
that veteran reps can't simply coast on past sales. Or it
can mean tailoring compensation systems to the type of
sale. For example, one of Aggreko North America's business lines, called Aggreko Process Services, provides engineering services to supplement the temperature control
equipment that the company rents to oil refineries
(among other customers). Reps who sell these offerings—
often involving a long and complex sales cycle—don't
work on straight commission. Instead, they are paid a relatively high salary plus a bonus based on achieving targets. Meanwhile, reps who sell less-complex rentals, such
as those to construction companies, earn a higher proportion of their compensation in commissions.

SALES FORCE DEPLOYMENT

How a company goes to market—how it organizes and
deploys not just its reps but its sales, support, marketing, and delivery resources—is a critical part of the sales
process. Any company that has watched its territory-
based sales reps migrate down-market toward easy sales
rather than profitable ones is facing a deployment problem. Its resources simply aren't being put where they can
generate the greatest return.

One simple way to fix a deployment issue is to create
a demand map of the market using segmentation information and then to compare it with your deployment

map. The point is to substitute data for gut feel to identify where the best prospects are and to synchronize that
information with the companies that sales reps actually
call on.

But an analytical approach to deployment goes well
beyond simply matching up reps with particular
prospects. Best-practice companies also typically bench-
mark themselves on whether approaches to sales are
paired up with the right customers.

Most companies, for example, utilize a range of sales
channels: enterprise or other direct sales, inside sales, the
Internet, dealers or value-added resellers, and so on.
Having access to detailed information about the behavior and profitability of customer segments and micro-
segments allows sales executives to decide how best to
deploy these different resources. For instance, inquiries
about Aggreko North America's commodity rentals
are directed to the Internet or closed by telesales; inquiries about large consultative projects are sent to specialized sales reps. The ideal salesperson for the firm's
construction-related business, says company president
Walker, isn't necessarily a construction expert but a
rep who "knows how to make 50 sales calls a week" and
can close deals quickly. "The perfect rep for Aggreko's
refinery business," Walker continues, "is someone
who is comfortable with long sales cycles and complex,
technology-intensive solutions."

Another question that leading sales organizations ask
themselves is, Are the field reps spending as much time
as possible selling? When we measure salespeople's
"non-customer-facing time," we find that it often
amounts to more than half of their total hours. If sales
executives uncover that kind of problem, they have a
variety of tools at their disposal. They may be able to

channel some of the reps' administrative functions to support staff. They may want to reorganize territories to minimize time spent in transit. They also may simplify the systems that the reps are expected to deal with. Several years ago, sales executives at Cisco set a goal of reducing reps' nonselling time by a few hours a week and charged the IT department with making it happen. The improvement led to several hundred million dollars in additional revenue.

All four of the levers help increase sales force productivity. What's most interesting, however, is that they seem to have the greatest effect on lower-ranked performers and so narrow the gap between top performers and everyone else. When we studied the results of a systematic sales force effectiveness program launched in several branches of a large Korean financial services provider, we found that the branches experienced a 44% rise in weekly sales volume, compared with a 6% decline in other branches. The top quartile of customer-service reps increased their product sales by 6%, the second quartile by 59%, the third quartile by 77%, and the bottom quartile by an astonishing 149%. A study of a comparable program in the Korean offices of another global financial-services firm found similar, though not identical, results. Increases in assets under management ranged from 2% in the top quartile to 33% in the second quartile to 54% in the third quartile, with the lowest quartile registering a 44% increase.

Beyond Best Practice

Finding, attracting, and holding on to talented salespeople is more difficult than ever. And companies can no longer afford to depend on them the way they once did. "It's gotten incredibly expensive to hire stars from competitors," acknowledges Citigroup's Thomson. Relying on the persuasive or relationship-building powers of a small group of talented individuals is simply insufficient for predictable, sustainable growth. (See the sidebar "A New Role for Rainmakers" at the end of this article.)

Fortunately, sales executives like Bob Brody don't need to depend exclusively on rainmakers to achieve their numbers. They can get much more out of their entire sales force by using a hard-nosed, scientific approach to sales force effectiveness. Like any science, of course, this one is evolving. The tools and processes we have described are today's best practice, but in a few years, they will almost certainly be standard operating procedure for any company that hopes to compete effectively in the global marketplace.

TOPSales: A Science-Driven Approach

IN TODAY'S SELLING environment, it's not enough to rely on your star reps and hope for the best. Any sales organization that wants to boost productivity should use a scientific approach to selling based on a set of four levers (which make up the abbreviation TOPSales).

Targeted offerings

TAILOR YOUR OFFERINGS to meet the needs of each segment, and make sure reps are selling the right wares to the right prospects.

Optimized automation, tools, and procedure

BOLSTER YOUR TECHNOLOGY TOOLS with disciplined sales management processes, such as detailed pipeline discussions, systematic account and territory plan reviews based on standard guidelines, defined lead distribution processes with tracking throughout the sales cycle for both reps and partners, and electronic dashboards for reps and territories.

Performance management

MEASURE AND MANAGE INPUTS, such as pipeline metrics and competitive installations you want to target, but reward based on outputs. Calculate the time it will take new reps to begin generating revenue, and factor that in to your sales planning. Provide training and tools to reduce that time. Incorporate metrics, incentives, and skill development into compensation systems to reward high-performing reps.

Sales force deployment

DISTRIBUTE YOUR SALES resources systematically, matching sales approaches and channels to the needs and challenges of each customer segment. Create teams for complex sales, and provide reps with support to help maximize their productivity.

A New Role for Rainmakers

HIGH-PERFORMING SALESPEOPLE have always delivered the goods for their businesses. Can they be helpful in other ways as well? While we believe there is no substitute for the right segmentation strategy, processes, leadership, tools, and incentives, we also think that companies often fail to take full advantage of their top salespeople.

But that may be changing. Today, relationship sales consultants such as Andrew Sobel (coauthor of *Clients for Life*) and Tim Leishman (of consulting firm Leishman Performance Strategy) are taking a page from cognitive science and showing that it's possible to teach the underlying behaviors of top salespeople. In our experience, the best companies are aiming to do this instead of first searching for new stars. They are defining a new role for their rainmakers as collegial mentors who can impart what appear to be instinctual relationship-building skills. These firms are also having their rainmakers teach new hires how to break customer-winning behaviors down into actions they can adapt to their own personalities.

One pharmaceutical services company took just such an approach: It created a three-step training initiative that paired sales stars (who brought in about half the company's revenues) with new hires. During the "first steps" phase, the stars educated the newcomers about the market and took them on sales calls so they could observe firsthand how the high-performing veterans worked. During the "walking" phase, the newcomers made the calls— but the stars joined them, watched them, and offered tips and feedback. For the remainder of the year (the "running" phase), the stars met regularly with the newcomers to discuss progress and share ideas. The approach took about a year and capitalized not only on the high performers' desire to share their skills but also on their desire to earn: They received a 1% commission on all revenue brought in by the mentee during the yearlong program.

Originally published in September 2006
Reprint R0609H

How to Pitch a Brilliant Idea

KIMBERLY D. ELSBACH

Executive Summary

COMING UP with creative ideas is easy; selling them
to strangers is hard. Entrepreneurs, sales executives,
and marketing managers often go to great lengths to
demonstrate how their new concepts are practical and
profitable—only to be rejected by corporate decision
makers who don't seem to understand the value of the
ideas. Why does this happen?

Having studied Hollywood executives who assess
screenplay pitches, the author says the person on the
receiving end—the "catcher"—tends to gauge the pitcher's
creativity as well as the proposal itself. An impression of
the pitcher's ability to come up with workable ideas can
quickly and permanently overshadow the catcher's feelings about an idea's worth. To determine whether these
observations apply to business settings beyond Hollywood, the author attended product design, marketing,

and venture-capital pitch sessions and conducted interviews with executives responsible for judging new ideas. The results in those environments were similar to her observations in Hollywood, she says.

Catchers subconsciously categorize successful pitchers as *showrunners* (smooth and professional), *artists* (quirky and unpolished), or *neophytes* (inexperienced and naive). The research also reveals that catchers tend to respond well when they believe they are participating in an idea's development. As Oscar-winning writer, director, and producer Oliver Stone puts it, screenwriters pitching an idea should "pull back and project what he needs onto your idea in order to make the story whole for him."

To become a successful pitcher, portray yourself as one of the three creative types and engage your catchers in the creative process. By finding ways to give your catchers a chance to shine, you sell yourself as a likable collaborator.

COMING UP WITH creative ideas is easy; selling them to strangers is hard. All too often, entrepreneurs, sales executives, and marketing managers go to great lengths to show how their new business plans or creative concepts are practical and high margin—only to be rejected by corporate decision makers who don't seem to understand the real value of the ideas. Why does this happen?

It turns out that the problem has as much to do with the seller's traits as with an idea's inherent quality. The person on the receiving end tends to gauge the pitcher's creativity as well as the proposal itself. And judgments about the pitcher's ability to come up with workable ideas can quickly and permanently overshadow perceptions of the idea's worth. We all like to think that people judge us carefully and objectively on our merits. But the fact is, they rush to place us into neat little categories— they stereotype us. So the first thing to realize when you're preparing to make a pitch to strangers is that your audience is going to put you into a box. And they're going to do it really fast. Research suggests that humans can categorize others in less than 150 milliseconds. Within 30 minutes, they've made lasting judgments about your character.

These insights emerged from my lengthy study of the $50 billion U.S. film and television industry. Specifically, I worked with 50 Hollywood executives involved in assessing pitches from screenwriters. Over the course of six years, I observed dozens of 30-minute pitches in which the screenwriters encountered the "catchers" for the first time. In interviewing and observing the pitchers and catchers, I was able to discern just how quickly assessments of creative potential are made in these high-stakes exchanges. (The deals that arise as a result of successful screenplay pitches are often multimillion-dollar projects, rivaling in scope the development of new car models by Detroit's largest automakers and marketing campaigns by New York's most successful advertising agencies.) To determine whether my observations applied to business settings beyond Hollywood, I attended a variety of product-design, marketing, and venture-capital pitch sessions and conducted interviews with executives responsible for judging creative, high-stakes ideas from pitchers previously unknown to them. In those environments, the results were remarkably similar to what I had seen in the movie business.

People on the receiving end of pitches have no formal, verifiable, or objective measures for assessing that elusive trait, creativity. Catchers—even the expert ones—therefore apply a set of subjective and often inaccurate criteria very early in the encounter, and from that point on, the tone is set. If a catcher detects subtle cues indicating that the pitcher isn't creative, the proposal is toast. But that's not the whole story. I've discovered that catchers tend to respond well if they are made to feel that they are participating in an idea's development.

The pitchers who do this successfully are those who tend to be categorized by catchers into one of three prototypes. I call them the *showrunner,* the *artist,* and the *neophyte.* Showrunners come off as professionals who combine creative inspiration with production know-how. Artists appear to be quirky and unpolished and to prefer the world of creative ideas to quotidian reality. Neophytes tend to be—or act as if they were—young, inexperienced, and naive. To involve the audience in the creative process, showrunners deliberately level the power differential between themselves and their catchers; artists invert the differential; and neophytes exploit it. If you're a pitcher, the bottom-line implication is this: By successfully projecting yourself as one of the three creative types and getting your catcher to view himself or herself as a creative collaborator, you can improve your chances of selling an idea.

My research also has implications for those who buy ideas: Catchers should beware of relying on stereotypes. It's all too easy to be dazzled by pitchers who ultimately can't get their projects off the ground, and it's just as easy to overlook the creative individuals who can make good on their ideas. That's why it's important for the catcher to test every pitcher, a matter we'll return to in the following pages.

The Sorting Hat

In the late 1970s, psychologists Nancy Cantor and Walter Mischel, then at Stanford University, demonstrated that we all use sets of stereotypes—what they called "person prototypes"—to categorize strangers in the first moments of interaction. Though such instant typecasting is arguably unfair, pattern matching is so firmly hardwired into human psychology that only conscious discipline can counteract it.

Yale University creativity researcher Robert Sternberg contends that the prototype matching we use to assess originality in others results from our implicit belief that creative people possess certain traits—unconventionality, for example, as well as intuitiveness, sensitivity, narcissism, passion, and perhaps youth. We develop these stereotypes through direct and indirect experiences with people known to be creative, from personally interacting with the 15-year-old guitar player next door to hearing stories about Pablo Picasso.

When a person we don't know pitches an idea to us, we search for visual and verbal matches with those implicit models, remembering only the characteristics that identify the pitcher as one type or another. We subconsciously award points to people we can easily identify as having creative traits; we subtract points from those who are hard to assess or who fit negative stereotypes.

In hurried business situations in which executives must evaluate dozens of ideas in a week, or even a day, catchers are rarely willing to expend the effort necessary to judge an idea more objectively. Like Harry Potter's Sorting Hat, they classify pitchers in a matter of seconds. They use negative stereotyping to rapidly identify the no-go ideas. All you have to do is fall into one of four common negative stereotypes, and the pitch session will be over before it has begun. (For more on these stereotypes, see the sidebar "How to Kill Your Own Pitch" at the end of this article.) In fact, many such sessions are strictly a process of elimination; in my experience, only 1% of ideas make it beyond the initial pitch.

Unfortunately for pitchers, type-based elimination is easy, because negative impressions tend to be more salient and memorable than positive ones. To avoid fast elimination, successful pitchers—only 25% of those I have observed—turn the tables on the catchers by enrolling them in the creative process. These pitchers exude passion for their ideas and find ways to give catchers a chance to shine. By doing so, they induce the catchers to judge them as likable collaborators. Oscar-winning writer, director, and producer Oliver Stone told me that the invitation to collaborate on an idea is a "seduction." His advice to screenwriters pitching an idea to a producer is to "pull back and project what he needs onto your idea in order to make the story whole for him." The three types of successful pitchers have their own techniques for doing this, as we'll see.

The Showrunner

In the corporate world, as in Hollywood, showrunners combine creative thinking and passion with what Sternberg and Todd Lubart, authors of *Defying the Crowd: Cultivating Creativity in a Culture of Conformity*, call "practical intelligence"—a feel for which ideas are likely to contribute to the business. Showrunners tend to display charisma and wit in pitching, say, new design concepts to marketing, but they also demonstrate enough technical know-how to convince catchers that the ideas can be developed according to industry-standard practices and within resource constraints. Though they may not have the most or the best ideas, showrunners are those rare people in organizations who see the majority of their concepts fully implemented.

An example of a showrunner is the legendary kitchen-gadget inventor and pitchman Ron Popeil. Perfectly coiffed and handsome, Popeil is a combination design master and ringmaster. In his *New Yorker* account of Popeil's phenomenally successful Ronco Showtime Rotisserie & BBQ, Malcolm Gladwell described how Popeil fuses entertainment skills—he enthusiastically showcases the product as an innovation that will "change your life"—with business savvy. For his television spots, Popeil makes sure that the chickens are roasted to exactly the resplendent golden brown that looks best on camera. And he designed the rotisserie's glass front to reduce glare, so that to the home cook, the revolving, dripping chickens look just as they do on TV.

The first Hollywood pitcher I observed was a showrunner. The minute he walked into the room, he scored points with the studio executive as a creative type, in part because of his new, pressed jeans, his fashionable black turtleneck, and his nice sport coat. The clean hair draping his shoulders showed no hint of gray. He had come to pitch a weekly television series based on the legend of Robin Hood. His experience as a marketer was apparent; he opened by mentioning an earlier TV series of his that had been based on a comic book. The pitcher remarked that the series had enjoyed some success as a marketing franchise, spawning lunch boxes, bath toys, and action figures.

Showrunners create a level playing field by engaging the catcher in a kind of knowledge duet. They typically begin by getting the catcher to respond to a memory or some other subject with which the showrunner is familiar. Consider this give-and-take:

PITCHER: *Remember Errol Flynn's Robin Hood?*
CATCHER: *Oh, yeah. One of my all-time favorites as a kid.*
PITCHER: *Yes, it was classic. Then, of course, came Costner's version.*
CATCHER: *That was much darker. And it didn't evoke as much passion as the original.*
PITCHER: *But the special effects were great.*
CATCHER: *Yes, they were.*
PITCHER: *That's the twist I want to include in this new series.*
CATCHER: *Special effects?*
PITCHER: *We're talking a science fiction version of Robin Hood. Robin has a sorcerer in his band of merry men who can conjure up all kinds of scary and wonderful spells.*
CATCHER: *I love it!*

The pitcher sets up his opportunity by leading the catcher through a series of shared memories and viewpoints. Specifically, he engages the catcher by asking him to recall and comment on familiar movies. With each response, he senses and then builds on the catcher's knowledge and interest, eventually guiding the catcher to the core idea by using a word ("twist") that's common to the vocabularies of both producers and screenwriters.

Showrunners also display an ability to improvise, a quality that allows them to adapt if a pitch begins to go awry. Consider the dynamic between the creative director of an ad agency and a prospective client, a major television sports network. As Mallorre Dill reported in a 2001 *Adweek* article on award-winning advertising campaigns, the network's VP of marketing was seeking help with a new campaign for coverage of the upcoming professional basketball season, and the ad agency was invited to make a pitch. Prior to the meeting, the network executive stressed to the agency that the campaign would have to appeal to local markets across the United States while achieving "street credibility" with avid fans.

The agency's creative director and its art director pitched the idea of digitally inserting two average teenagers into video of an NBA game. Initially, the catcher frowned on the idea, wondering aloud if viewers would find it arrogant and aloof. So the agency duo adlibbed a rap that one teen could recite after scoring on all-star Shaquille O'Neal: "I'm fresh like a can of picante. And I'm deeper than Dante in the circles of hell." The catcher was taken aback at first; then he laughed. Invited to participate in the impromptu rap session, the catcher began inserting his own lines. When the fun was over, the presenters repitched their idea with a slight variation— inserting the teenagers into videos of home-team games for local markets—and the account was sold to the tune of hundreds of thousands of dollars.

Real showrunners are rare—only 20% of the successful pitchers I observed would qualify. Consequently, they are in high demand, which is good news for pitchers who can demonstrate the right combination of talent and expertise.

The Artist

Artists, too, display single-minded passion and enthusiasm about their ideas, but they are less slick and conformist in their dress and mannerisms, and they tend to be shy or socially awkward. As one Hollywood producer told me, "The more shy a writer seems, the better you think the writing is, because you assume they're living in their internal world." Unlike show-runners, artists appear to have little or no knowledge of, or even interest in, the details of implementation. Moreover, they invert the power differential by completely commanding the catcher's imagination. Instead of engaging the catcher in a duet, they put the audience in thrall to the content. Artists are particularly adept at conducting what physicists call "thought experiments," inviting the audience into imaginary worlds.

One young screenwriter I observed fit the artist type to perfection. He wore black leather pants and a torn T-shirt, several earrings in each ear, and a tattoo on his slender arm. His hair was rumpled, his expression was brooding: Van Gogh meets Tim Burton. He cared little about the production details for the dark, violent cartoon series he imagined; rather, he was utterly absorbed by the unfolding story. He opened his pitch like this: "Picture what happens when a bullet explodes inside someone's brain. Imagine it in slow motion. There is the shattering blast, the tidal wave of red, the acrid smell of gunpowder. That's the opening scene in this animated sci-fi flick." He then proceeded to lead his catchers through an exciting, detailed narrative of his film, as a master storyteller would. At the end, the executives sat back, smiling, and told the writer they'd like to go ahead with his idea.

In the business world, artists are similarly noncon-formist. Consider Alan, a product designer at a major packaged-foods manufacturer. I observed Alan in a meeting with business-development executives he'd never met. He had come to pitch an idea based on the premise that children like to play with their food. The proposal was for a cereal with pieces that interlocked in such a way that children could use them for building things, Legos style. With his pocket-protected laboratory coat and horn-rimmed glasses, Alan looked very much the absent-minded professor. As he entered the conference room where the suited-and-tied executives at his company had assembled, he hung back, apparently uninterested in the Power-Point slides or the marketing and revenue projections of the business-development experts. His appearance and reticence spoke volumes about him. His type was unmistakable.

When it was Alan's turn, he dumped four boxes of prototype cereal onto the mahogany conference table, to the stunned silence of the executives. Ignoring protocol, he began constructing an elaborate fort, all the while talking furiously about the qualities of the corn flour that kept the pieces and the structure together. Finally, he challenged the executives to see who could build the tallest tower. The executives so enjoyed the demonstration that they green-lighted Alan's project.

While artists—who constituted about 40% of the successful pitchers I observed—are not as polished as show-runners, they are the most creative of the three types. Unlike showrunners and neophytes, artists are fairly transparent. It's harder to fake the part. In other words, they don't play to type; they *are* the type. Indeed, it is very difficult for someone who is not an artist to pretend to be one, because genuineness is what makes the artist credible.

The Neophyte

Neophytes are the opposite of showrunners. Instead of displaying their expertise, they plead ignorance. Neophytes score points for daring to do the impossible, something catchers see as refreshing. Unencumbered by tradition or past successes, neophytes present themselves as eager learners. They consciously exploit the power differential between pitcher and catcher by asking directly and boldly for help—not in a desperate way, but with the confidence of a brilliant favorite, a talented student seeking sage advice from a beloved mentor.

Consider the case of one neophyte pitcher I observed, a young, ebullient screenwriter who had just returned from his first trip to Japan. He wanted to develop a show about an American kid (like himself) who travels to Japan to learn to play *taiko* drums, and he brought his drums and sticks into the pitch session. The fellow looked as though he had walked off the set of *Doogie Howser, M.D.* With his infectious smile, he confided to his catchers that he was not going to pitch them a typical show, "mainly because I've never done one. But I think my inexperience here might be a blessing."

He showed the catchers a variety of drumming moves, then asked one person in his audience to help him come up with potential camera angles—such as looking out from inside the drum or viewing it from overhead—inquiring how these might play on the screen. When the catcher got down on his hands and knees to show the neophyte a particularly "cool" camera angle, the pitch turned into a collaborative teaching session. Ignoring his lunch appointment, the catcher spent the next half hour offering suggestions for weaving the story of the young drummer into a series of taiko performances in which artistic camera angles and imaginative lighting and sound would be used to mirror the star's emotions.

Many entrepreneurs are natural neophytes. Lou and Sophie McDermott, two sisters from Australia, started the Savage Sisters sportswear line in the late 1990s. Former gymnasts with petite builds and spunky personalities, they cart-wheeled into the clothing business with no formal training in fashion or finance. Instead, they relied heavily on their enthusiasm and optimism and a keen curiosity about the fine points of retailing to get a start in the highly competitive world of teen fashion. On their shopping outings at local stores, the McDermott sisters studied merchandising and product placement— all the while asking store owners how they got started, according to the short documentary film *Cutting Their Own Cloth.*

The McDermott sisters took advantage of their inexperience to learn all they could. They would ask a store owner to give them a tour of the store, and they would pose dozens of questions: "Why do you buy this line and not the other one? Why do you put this dress here and not there? What are your customers like? What do they ask for most?" Instead of being annoying, the McDermotts were charming, friendly, and fun, and the flattered retailers enjoyed being asked to share their knowledge. Once they had struck up a relationship with a retailer, the sisters would offer to bring in samples for the store to test. Eventually, the McDermotts parlayed what they had learned into enough knowledge to start their own retail line. By engaging the store owners as teachers, the McDermotts were able to build a network of expert mentors who wanted to see the neophytes win. Thus neophytes, who constitute about 40% of successful pitchers, achieve their gains largely by sheer force of personality.

Which of the three types is most likely to succeed?
Overwhelmingly, catchers look for showrunners, though
artists and neophytes can win the day through enchant-
ment and charm. From the catcher's perspective, however, show-runners can also be the most dangerous of all
pitchers, because they are the most likely to blind
through glitz.

Catchers Beware

When business executives ask me for my insights about
creativity in Hollywood, one of the first questions they
put to me is, "Why is there so much bad television?"
After hearing the stories I've told here, they know the
answer: Hollywood executives too often let themselves
be wooed by positive stereotypes—particularly that
of the showrunner—rather than by the quality of the
ideas. Indeed, individuals who become adept at con-
veying impressions of creative potential, while lacking
the real thing, may gain entry into organizations and
reach prominence there based on their social influence
and impression-management skills, to the catchers'
detriment.

Real creativity isn't so easily classified. Researchers
such as Sternberg and Lubart have found that people's
implicit theories regarding the attributes of creative individuals are off the mark. Furthermore, studies have identified numerous personal attributes that facilitate practical creative behavior. For example, cognitive flexibility, a
penchant for diversity, and an orientation toward problem solving are signs of creativity; it simply isn't true that
creative types can't be down-to-earth.

Those who buy ideas, then, need to be aware that relying too heavily on stereotypes can cause them to over-

look creative individuals who can truly deliver the goods. In my interviews with studio executives and agents, I heard numerous tales of people who had developed reputations as great pitchers but who had trouble producing usable scripts. The same thing happens in business. One well-known example occurred in 1985, when Coca-Cola announced it was changing the Coke formula. Based on pitches from market researchers who had tested the sweeter, Pepsi-like "new Coke" in numerous focus groups, the company's top management decided that the new formula could effectively compete with Pepsi. The idea was a marketing disaster, of course. There was a huge backlash, and the company was forced to reintroduce the old Coke. In a later discussion of the case and the importance of relying on decision makers who are both good pitchers and industry experts, Roberto Goizueta, Coca-Cola's CEO at the time, said to a group of MBAs, in effect, that there's nothing so dangerous as a good pitcher with no real talent.

If a catcher senses that he or she is being swept away by a positive stereotype match, it's important to test the pitcher. Fortunately, assessing the various creative types is not difficult. In a meeting with a showrunner, for example, the catcher can test the pitcher's expertise and probe into past experiences, just as a skilled job interviewer would, and ask how the pitcher would react to various changes to his or her idea. As for artists and neophytes, the best way to judge their ability is to ask them to deliver a finished product. In Hollywood, smart catchers ask artists and neophytes for finished scripts before hiring them. These two types may be unable to deliver specifics about costs or implementation, but a proto-type can allow the catcher to judge quality, and it can provide a concrete basis for further discussion.

Finally, it's important to enlist the help of other people in vetting pitchers. Another judge or two can help a catcher weigh the pitcher's—and the idea's—pros and cons and help safeguard against hasty judgments.

One CEO of a Northern California design firm looks beyond the obvious earmarks of a creative type when hiring a new designer. She does this by asking not only about successful projects but also about work that failed and what the designer learned from the failures. That way, she can find out whether the prospect is capable of absorbing lessons well and rolling with the punches of an unpredictable work environment. The CEO also asks job prospects what they collect and read, as well as what inspires them. These kinds of clues tell her about the applicant's creative bent and thinking style. If an interviewee passes these initial tests, the CEO has the prospect work with the rest of her staff on a mock design project. These diverse interview tools give her a good indication about the prospect's ability to combine creativity and organizational skills, and they help her understand how well the applicant will fit into the group.

One question for pitchers, of course, might be, "How do I make a positive impression if I don't fit into one of the three creative stereotypes?" If you already have a reputation for delivering on creative promises, you probably don't need to disguise yourself as a showrunner, artist, or neophyte—a résumé full of successes is the best calling card of all. But if you can't rely on your reputation, you should at least make an attempt to match yourself to the type you feel most comfortable with, if only because it's necessary to get a foot in the catcher's door.

Another question might be, "What if I don't *want* the catcher's input into the development of my idea?" This aspect of the pitch is so important that you should make it a priority: Find a part of your proposal that you are willing to yield on and invite the catcher to come up with suggestions. In fact, my observations suggest that you should engage the catcher as soon as possible in the development of the idea. Once the catcher feels like a creative collaborator, the odds of rejection diminish.

Ultimately, the pitch will always remain an imperfect process for communicating creative ideas. But by being aware of stereotyping processes and the value of collaboration, both pitchers and catchers can understand the difference between a pitch and a hit.

How to Kill Your Own Pitch

BEFORE YOU EVEN GET to the stage in the pitch where the catcher categorizes you as a particular creative type, you have to avoid some dangerous pigeonholes: the four negative stereotypes that are guaranteed to kill a pitch. And take care, because negative cues carry more weight than positive ones.

The pushover would rather unload an idea than defend it. ("I could do one of these in red, or if you don't like that, I could do it in blue.") One venture capitalist I spoke with offered the example of an entrepreneur who was seeking funding for a computer networking start-up. When the VCs raised concerns about an aspect of the device, the pitcher simply offered to remove it from the design, leading the investors to suspect that the pitcher didn't really care about his idea.

The robot presents a proposal too formulaically, as if it had been memorized from a how-to book. Witness the entrepreneur who responds to prospective investors' questions about due diligence and other business details with canned answers from his PowerPoint talk.

The used-car salesman is that obnoxious, argumentative character too often deployed in consultancies and corporate sales departments. One vice president of marketing told me the story of an arrogant consultant who put in a proposal to her organization. The consultant's offer was vaguely intriguing, and she asked him to revise his bid slightly. Instead of working with her, he argued with her. Indeed, he tried selling the same package again and again, each time arguing why his proposal would produce the most astonishing bottom-line results the company had ever seen. In the end, she grew so tired of his wheedling insistence and inability to listen courteously to her feedback that she told him she wasn't interested in seeing any more bids from him.

The charity case is needy; all he or she wants is a job. I recall a freelance consultant who had developed a course for executives on how to work with independent screenwriters. He could be seen haunting the halls of production companies, knocking on every open door, giving the same pitch. As soon as he sensed he was being turned down, he began pleading with the catcher, saying he really, *really* needed to fill some slots to keep his workshop going.

Originally published in September 2003
Reprint R0309J

What Makes a Good Salesman

DAVID MAYER AND HERBERT M. GREENBERG

Executive Summary

DESPITE MILLIONS of dollars spent on combating the high turnover rate among insurance agents, the rate—approximately 50% within the first year and 80% within the first three years—had remained steady for the more than 35 years preceding the publication of Mayer and Greenberg's 1964 article. The authors devoted seven years of research to studying the problem of the ineffectiveness of large numbers of salespeople. They discovered flaws in the established methods of selection and revealed the two basic qualities that any good salesperson must have: empathy and ego drive.

Empathy, in this context, is the central ability to feel as other people do in order to sell them a product or service; a buyer who senses a salesperson's empathy will provide him with valuable feedback, which will in turn facilitate the sale. The authors define the second of the two qualities, ego drive, as the personal desire and need to make the sale—not because of the money to be gained but because the salesperson feels he *has* to. For sales reps with strong ego drives, every sale is a conquest that dramatically improves their self-perception. In the dynamic relationship between empathy and ego drive, each must work to reinforce the other.

Why did the executives that Mayer and Greenberg studied continue to hire salespeople who did not have the ability to perform well? The companies were hindered in the preselection process by flaws in the prevailing forms of aptitude testing. Test takers could easily give answers they knew the test givers wanted to hear, in part because the tests sought to identify particular psychological traits rather than the personality type most capable of selling.

M ORE THAN 35 YEARS AGO, the insurance industry embarked on an intensive program to solve the problem of costly, wasteful turnover among its agents. Estimates at that time indicated that there was a turnover of better than 50% within the first year and almost 80% within the first three years. After the expenditure of millions of dollars and 35 years of research, the turnover in the insurance industry remains approximately 50% within the first year and 80% within the first three years.

What is the cost of this turnover? Nearly incalculable. Consider:

- the substantial sums paid new salesmen as salary, draw on commission, expense accounts, and so

on, which are wasted when those salesmen fail
to sell;

• the staggering company costs, in time, money, and
energy, of recruiting, selecting, training, and supervis-
ing men who inherently do not have the ability to succeed; and

• the vast costs caused by lost sales, drop-outs, reduced
company reputation, poor morale, permanently
burned territory, and the like.

What accounts for this expensive inefficiency? Basically this: Companies have simply not known what
makes one man able to sell and another not. As Robert
N. McMurry has observed:

> A very high proportion of those engaged in selling can-
> not sell. . . . If American sales efficiency is to be maxi-
> mized and the appalling waste of money and manpower
> which exists today is to be minimized, a constructive
> analysis must be made of what selling really is and how
> its effectiveness can be enhanced. . . . We must look a
> good deal further—into the mysteries of personality and
> psychology—if we want real answers.[1]

It was the obvious need for a better method of sales
selection that led us to embark on seven years of field
research in this area. The article that follows is based on
the insights we gained as to the basic characteristics necessary for a salesman to be able to sell successfully. Con-
firming the fact that we are on the right track is the pre-
dictive power of the selection instrument (battery of
tests) that we developed out of the same research; see the
exhibit "How Well an Instrument Measuring Empathy
and Ego Drive Predicted Sales Success."

How Well an Instrument Measuring Empathy and Ego Drive Predicted Sales Success

Number of men predicted for each group*	Data at end of (months)	Actual sales performance (number of men who reached each quarter of sales force)				
		Top half		Bottom half		
		Top/ quarter	2nd/ quarter	3rd/ quarter	Bottom/ quarter	Quit or fired
In the Retail Automobile Industry						
A 34	6 mos.	17	13	1	0	3
	18	19	9	0	0	6
B 49	6	9	23	8	2	7
	18	10	19	8	0	12
C 60	6	0	9	20	14	17
	18	0	2	21	8	29
D 52	6	0	0	10	18	24
	18	0	0	9	7	36

In the Insurance Industry

		6 mos.					
A	22		13	4	1	0	4
		14	13	4	0	0	5
B	55	6	7	23	11	2	12
		14	11	20	7	1	16
C	56	6	1	5	19	12	19
		14	1	4	11	5	35
D	48	6	0	0	4	10	34
		14	0	0	3	4	41

In the Mutual Funds Industry

		6 mos.					
A	11	6	5	4	1	0	1
B	20	6	4	9	3	0	4
C	49	6	0	4	15	12	18
D	34	6	0	1	7	10	16

* Predictions made on basis of test, without seeing men or any records:

A means outstanding, top potential as a salesman, almost certain to succeed with high productivity.

B means recommended, good productivity, and can sometimes be designated as developable into an A.

C means not recommended, even though a C can under the right circumstances edge into becoming a low B.

D means absolutely not recommended; the applicant concerned has virtually no possibility of success.

Two Essentials

Our basic theory is that a good salesman must have at least two basic qualities: empathy and ego drive.

ABILITY TO FEEL

Empathy, the important central ability to feel as the other fellow does in order to be able to sell him a product or service, must be possessed in large measure. Having empathy does not necessarily mean being sympathetic. One can know what the other fellow feels without agreeing with that feeling. But a salesman simply cannot sell well without the invaluable and irreplaceable ability to get a powerful feedback from the client through empathy.

A parallel might be drawn in this connection between the old antiaircraft weapons and the new heat-attracted missiles. With the old type of ballistic weapon, the gunner would take aim at an airplane, correcting as best he could for windage and driftage, and then fire. If the shell missed by just a few inches because of a slight error in calculation or because the plane took evasive action, the miss might just as well have been by hundreds of yards for all the good it did.

This is the salesman with poor empathy. He aims at the target as best he can and proceeds along his sales track; but if his target—the customer—fails to perform as predicted, the sale is missed.

On the other hand, the new missiles, if they are anywhere near the target, become attracted to the heat of the target's engine, and regardless of its evasive action, they finally home in and hit their mark.

This is the salesman with good empathy. He senses the reactions of the customer and is able to adjust to these reactions. He is not simply bound by a prepared sales track, but he functions in terms of the real interaction between himself and the customer. Sensing what the customer is feeling, he is able to change pace, double back on his track, and make whatever creative modifications might be necessary to home in on the target and close the sale.

NEED TO CONQUER

The second of the basic qualities absolutely needed by a good salesman is a particular kind of *ego drive* that makes him want and need to make the sale in a personal or ego way, not merely for the money to be gained. His feeling must be that he *has* to make the sale; the customer is there to help him fulfill his personal need. In effect, to the top salesman, the sale—the conquest—provides a powerful means of enhancing his ego. His self-picture improves dramatically by virtue of conquest and diminishes with failure.

Because of the nature of all selling, the salesman will fail to sell more often than he will succeed. Thus, since failure tends to diminish his self-picture, his ego cannot be so weak that the poor self-picture continues for too long a time. Rather, the failure must act as a trigger—as a motivation toward greater efforts—that with success will bring the ego enhancement he seeks. A subtle balance must be found between (a) an ego partially weakened in precisely the right way to need a great deal of enhancement (the sale) and (b) an ego sufficiently strong to be motivated by failure but not to be shattered by it.

The salesman's empathy, coupled with his intense ego drive, enables him to home in on the target effectively and make the sale. He has the drive, the need to make the sale,

*and his empathy gives him the connecting tool with which
to do it.*

Synergistic Effects

In this discussion of the relationship of empathy and ego
drive to successful selling, we will treat these dynamic
factors as separate characteristics. Indeed, they are
separate in that someone can have a great deal of empathy and any level of ego drive—extremely strong to
extremely weak. Someone with poor empathy can also
have any level of ego drive. Yet, as determinants of sales
ability, empathy and ego drive act on and, in fact, reinforce each other.

The person with strong ego drive has maximum motivation to fully utilize whatever empathy he possesses.
Needing the sale, he is not likely to let his empathy spill
over and become sympathy. His ego need for the conquest is not likely to allow him to side with the customer;
instead, it spurs him on to use his knowledge of the customer fully to make the sale.

On the other hand, the person with little or no ego
drive is hardly likely to use his empathy in a persuasive
manner. He understands people and may know perfectly
well what things he might say to close the sale effectively,
but his understanding is apt to become sympathy. If he
does not need the conquest, his very knowledge of the
real needs of the potential customer may tell him that
the customer in fact should not buy. Since he does not
need the sale in an inner personal sense, he then may not
persuade the customer to buy. So we frequently say in
our evaluations of potential salesmen, "This man has fine
empathy, but he is not likely to use it persuasively—he
will not use it to close."

Thus, there is a dynamic relationship between empathy and ego drive. It takes a combination of the two, each working to reinforce the other—each enabling the other to be fully utilized—to make the successful salesman.

NEED FOR BALANCE

It calls for a very special, balanced ego to need the sale intensely and yet allow the salesman to look closely at the customer and fully benefit from an empathic perception of the customer's reactions and needs.

Thus, there are a number of possible permutations of empathy and drive. A man may have a high degree of both empathy and drive (*ED*), or little of either (*ed*), or two kinds of combinations in between (*Ed* and *eD*). For example:

ED—A salesman who has a great deal of both empathy and strong inner sales drive will be at or near the top of the sales force.

Ed—A salesman with fine empathy but too little drive may be a splendid person but will be unable to close his deals effectively. This is the "nice guy." Everyone likes him, and from all appearances he should turn out to be one of the best men on the force. He somehow "doesn't make it." People end up liking him but buying from the company down the street. He is often hired because he does have such fine personal qualities. Yet his closing ability is weak. He will get along with the customer, understand him, and bring him near the close; but he does not have that inner hunger to move the customer that final one foot to the actual sale. It is this last element of the sale—the close—that empathy alone cannot achieve and where the assertive quality of ego drive becomes the all-important essential.

eD—A salesman with much drive but too little empathy will bulldoze his way through to some sales, but he will miss a great many and will hurt his employer through his lack of understanding of people.

ed—A salesman without much empathy or drive should not actually be a salesman, although a great many present salesmen fall into this group. An employer would avoid much grief by finding this out in advance, before so much effort is spent in trying to hire, train, and spoon-feed a man who does not have within him the basic dynamics to be successful.

Failure of Tests

Since the selection of top salesmen is potentially of such enormous value, why, it might be asked, has there been so little success to date in developing methods to pre-select effectively?

For at least 50 years, psychologists have been working very hard in the area of testing. Almost every aspect of human personality, behavior, attitude, and ability has at one time or another come under the scrutiny of the tester. There have been some notable successes in testing, most especially perhaps in the IQ and mechanical-ability areas. Of late, personality testing, especially with the increasing use of projective techniques, has gained a certain level of sophistication. The area which has been to date most barren of real scientific success has been aptitude testing, where the aptitude consists of personality dynamics rather than simple mechanical abilities.

FOUR REASONS

The ability to sell, an exceedingly human and totally nonmechanical aptitude, has resisted attempts to measure it effectively. The reasons for this failure up until now are many, but there appear to be four basic causes for sales aptitude test failure.

1. **Tests have been looking for interest, not ability.** The concept that a man's interest is equatable to his ability is perhaps the single largest cause of test failure. Thus, tests have been developed through asking questions of successful salesmen or successful people in other fields, with the assumption that if an applicant expresses the same kind of interest pattern as an established salesman, he too will be a successful salesman.

   This assumption is wrong on its face. Psychologically, interest does not equal aptitude. Even if someone is interested in exactly the same specific things as Mickey Mantle or Willie Mays, this of course does not in any way indicate the possession of a similar baseball skill. Equally, the fact that an individual might have the same interest pattern as a successful salesman does not mean that he can sell. Even if he wants to sell, it does not mean that he *can* sell.

2. **Tests have been eminently "fakable."** When an individual is applying for a job, he obviously will attempt to tell the potential employer whatever he thinks the employer wants to hear. Given a certain amount of intelligence, the applicant will know that he should say he would "rather be a salesman than a librarian," regardless of his real preference. He knows that he should say he would "rather be with people than at home reading a good book," that he "prefers talking to a PTA group to listening to good music," or that he would "rather lead a group discussion than be a forest ranger."

There are manuals on the market on how to beat
sales aptitude tests, but, even without such a manual,
the average intelligent person can quickly see what
is sought and then give the tester what the tester
wants. Thus, the tests may simply succeed in negatively screening those who are so unintelligent that
they are unable to see the particular response pattern
sought. In other words, since they are too dull to
fake, they may be screened out. The perceptive interviewer, however, is likely to notice this kind of stu-
pidity even more quickly than the tests do, and he
can probably do a better job of this negative screening than the average fakable test.

3. **Tests have favored group conformity, not individual creativity.** Recent critics of psychological testing
   decry the testers who are seeking conformity and the
   standardized ways in which they judge applicants for
   sales and other occupations. This criticism is all too
   valid. The creative thinker, the impulsive free spirit,
   the original, imaginative, hard-driving individual is
   often screened out by tests that demand rigid adherence to convention—an adherence, in fact, that bor-
   ders on a passive acceptance of authority, a fear of
   anything that might in any way upset the applecart
   of bureaucratic order. Paradoxically, this fearful, cau-
   tious, authoritarian conformist, although he might
   make a good civil servant, or even a fair controller or
   paperwork administrative executive, would never
   make a successful salesman.

Many of these tests not only fail to select good salesmen, but they may actually screen out the really top
producers because of their creativity, impulsiveness,
or originality—characteristics that most tests down-

grade as strangeness or weakness. We discovered a situation of this type recently in working with a client: A company in the Southwest embarked on an intensive recruiting effort for salesmen. We began receiving the tests of a number of applicants. These tests all appeared to follow a certain pattern. The men were not quite recommendable, and all for about the same reason—a definite lack of ego drive. For the most part, they had some empathy, and without exception they had good verbal ability, but none had the intense inner need for the sale that we look for in a productive salesman.

After about 20 such tests came through our office, we questioned the sales manager as to what criteria he was using for screening the men who took the test. We found that before he gave the applicants our test, he had them take the sales aptitude test that had been developed by his company some years before. Those men who scored high on that test were given our test.

We had previously analyzed that company's test and found it to be a fairly good verbal abilities measure, and to some extent a measure of intelligence and insight. Men with strong ego drive could not as a rule score near the top of that test. And so the very men with the quality we were seeking—strong ego drive— were actually screened out. We then asked the sales manager not to use that test but to screen only for credit reference and general appearance, and to give our test to those who passed this simple screening. After that we began seeing the expected number of "A" and "B" recommendable applicants—about one man in every five.

4. **Tests have tried to isolate fractional traits rather than to reveal the whole dynamics of the man.**
Most personality and aptitude tests are totally traitological in their construction and approach. They see personality as a series or "bundle" of piecemeal traits. Thus, someone may be high in "sociability" while being low in "self-sufficiency" and "dominance." Someone else may be high in "personal relations" but low in "cooperativeness." Somehow, the whole (or the gestalt) gets lost. The dynamic interaction that is personality, as viewed by most modern-day psychologists, is buried in a series of fractionalized, mathematically separable traits.

Thus, it is said that the salesman, somewhat like the Boy Scout, should be very "sociable," "dominant," "friendly," "responsible," "honest," and "loyal." The totality—the dynamics within the person that will permit him to sell successfully—is really lost sight of. Clearly, someone may be "sociable," "responsible," and so on, but still be a very poor salesman.

In our research we attempted to bypass traits and to go directly to the central dynamisms that we believed were basic to sales ability: empathy and ego drive. By seeking these deeper, more central, characteristics, we immediately reduced the possibility of faking, since the respondent would find it extremely difficult to determine what *in fact* was being sought. Needless to say, the importance of interest as a variable has been reduced sharply, and the conformity factor has been completely subordinated to the basic central characteristics being measured. Thus, rather than starting with the question, "How do salesmen collectively answer certain items?" we began with the question, "What makes a really fine salesman?" and then, "How do you discover these human characteristics?"

This use of central dynamics rather than traits, with its corollary implications, has produced what we believe to be a positive method of predicting sales success that is advanced beyond what has been done to date.

Fallacy of Experience

Many sales executives feel that the type of selling in their industry (and even in their particular company) is somehow completely special and unique. This is true to an extent. There is no question that a data-processing equipment salesman needs somewhat different training and background than does an automobile salesman. Differences in requirements are obvious, and whether or not the applicant meets the special qualifications for a particular job can easily be seen in the applicant's biography or readily measured. What is not so easily seen, however, are the basic sales dynamics we have been discussing, which permit an individual to sell successfully, almost regardless of what he is selling.

To date, we have gained experience with more than 7,000 salesmen of tangibles as well as intangibles, in wholesale as well as retail selling, big-ticket and little-ticket items. And the dynamics of success remain approximately the same in all cases. Sales ability is fundamental, more so than the product being sold. Long before he comes to know the product, mostly during his childhood and growing-up experience, the future successful salesman is developing the human qualities essential for selling. Thus, when emphasis is placed on experience, and experience counts more than such essentials as empathy and drive, what is accomplished can only be called the *inbreeding of mediocrity*.

We have found that the experienced person who is pirated from a competitor is most often piratable simply because he is not succeeding well with that competitor. He feels that somehow he can magically do better with the new company. This is rarely true. He remains what he is, mediocre, or worse. What companies need is a greater willingness to seek individuals with basic sales potential in the general marketplace. Experience is more or less easily gained, but real sales ability is not at all so easily gained.

Among butchers, coal miners, steelworkers, and even the unemployed there are many—perhaps *one in ten*—who, whether they themselves know it or not, possess the ability to be an A, top-producing salesman; and at least one in five would be on a B or better level for most types of selling. Many of these are potentially far better salesmen than some who have accumulated many years of experience. The case of "Big Jim," as we shall call him, is a good example: All we knew about Jim at first was that he had walked into the showroom of one of our automobile clients in response to its ad and had taken our test. We reported that he was the only A in the group, and strongly recommended that he be hired. There was shocked silence at the other end of the telephone. We were then told that his test had been included as a joke.

As it was described to us, he had ambled into the showroom one morning wearing dungarees, an old polo shirt, and sneakers. He had then gone on to proclaim, "I sure do hanker to sell them there cars." The dealer had included his test just to get a laugh, or perhaps to see if we were sufficiently alert to weed him out. The man had never sold a car or anything else in his life and had neither the appearance nor the background that would indicate that he ever could sell anything.

Today he is one of the dealer's best salesmen. Soon after he started working, he "hankered to see that there Seattle World's Fair" and sold enough cars in the first week of the month to give him money to get there and spend two weeks. On his return he made enough money in the last week of the month to equal the staff's monthly average.

Obviously, most men down from the hills wearing dungarees and sneakers are not going to be top salesmen. Some, however, may be, and their lack of experience in no way reduces the possibility that they have the inner dynamics of which fine top producers are made. It is equally obvious that a great many men who present a fine appearance, a "good front," do not turn out to be top salesmen. The real question—and always the first question—is, "Does this man have the basic inner dynamics to sell successfully?"

BACKGROUND BLINDNESS

Putting emphasis on experience often works in another way to reduce sales effectiveness. A company grows used to seeing its men in various job "slots," in certain departments, limited to special kinds of experience. Such men may be doing a satisfactory job where they are. But it frequently happens that the blind habit of "special experience" has kept the company from using the man in a more effective and appropriate way. For instance: A western company in the leasing business wanted us to evaluate a branch employing 42 men to determine why there had been a mediocre level of sales activity, why there had been some difficulties among the men, and whether some of the 42 should possibly be let go. After looking at the test of each person, we did an "X-ray" of the branch; that is, following the table of organization, we evaluated the staff, department by department, especially in terms of who was working with, over, and under whom, pointing out the strengths and weaknesses of each department.

Virtually all the men on the staff were found to be worth keeping on, but a good third were suggested for job shifts to other departments. Thus, the person with greatest sales ability, together with a great deal of managerial ability (by no means the same thing), was found in the accounting department. But that job did not completely satisfy him. He has since become the new branch sales manager, a more appropriate use of his considerable abilities.

One of the older men, though rated an adequate B salesman, was evaluated as an A office manager. He had good empathy, but not the strongest ego drive, which was why he was a B rather than an A salesman. But on the managerial side, he had the ability to handle details, relatively rare for a salesperson; he was able to delegate authority and make decisions fairly rapidly and well. These qualities, plus his good empathy, gave him excellent potential as a manager, but not as sales manager, for his only moderate drive would have hurt him in the latter position. As office administrative manager, the position he was moved up into, he has performed solidly.

The former office administrative manager, a man well able to handle details reliably and responsibly, but with little empathy (and thus unable to deal understandingly with his office staff), was moved laterally into the accounting department, an area in which he had had some previous experience, and where he could carefully deal with and manage details rather than people.

Thus, what counts more than experience is the man's basic inner abilities. Each present employee, as well as each new applicant, should be placed in the area where he can be most creative and productive.

Role of Training

The steelworker, the coal miner, the displaced textile worker, or for that matter even "Big Jim," regardless of how much real sales ability each possesses, cannot suddenly start selling insurance, mutual funds, electronics equipment, or automobiles. Each one will need training. Companies have spent very large sums of money in developing effective training programs. When they are working with a man with potential, these training programs can and do bring out this potential and develop an excellent salesman. Without sound training, even A-level salesmen are seriously limited.

Yet how often have men gone through long and expensive training programs only to fail totally when put out into the field? When this happens, the trainer, and perhaps the training program itself, is blamed and sometimes even discarded. But most often it is neither the trainer nor the training program that is at fault; rather, it is the fact that they were given the impossible task of turning a sow's ear into a silk purse. The most skilled diamond polisher, given a piece of coal, can only succeed in creating a highly polished piece of coal; but given the roughest type of uncut diamond, he can indeed turn it into the most precious stone. Here is a case in point: About three years ago, a company in the Northeast installed an especially fine training program, in which a great deal of money was invested. At the end of two years, the results of this program were appraised. It was found that sales had not increased beyond what might normally be expected in that industry during that period of time. The investment in the training program seemed to have been a total waste. The entire training program was therefore dropped. Six months later, we were asked by management to test and evaluate the present sales force and to try to determine why the training program, so highly recommended, had failed so badly.

The reason was immediately apparent. Out of a sales force of 18 men, there was only one rating A, and his sales actually had improved after the training program. Two others were B-level salesmen, and they too had improved to some extent with training. The remaining 15 men were "C" and "D" salesmen who should not have been selling in the first place. They simply did not have the potential of good salespeople. They were rigid, opinionated, and for the most part seriously lacking in empathy. This type of man rarely responds to training, no matter how thoroughgoing the program. This was an obvious case of trying to make silk purses out of 15 assorted sow's ears.

The role of training is clear. It is vital. In today's highly competitive market it is most important to bring every employee up to his maximum potential of productivity. Efficiency in training, using the best of modern methods, is necessary to do this. But training can succeed only if selection succeeds. Good raw silk must be provided first, before the training department can be expected to produce the silk purses. Just as few manufacturers would allow their products to be produced on the basis of rough estimates of size and weight, but would demand scientific control of these basic characteristics, so too must the process of selection be made more scientific and accurate.

The role of the salesman is so vital to the success of a company that it is amazing to these writers how little stress industry has placed on selecting the best raw material. To sell effectively in the U.S. market of today, a salesman needs to have empathy. To sell effectively in the foreign market, crossing cultural lines, requires even more empathy. And marketing goods and services anywhere calls for a great deal of ego drive. The U.S. Department of Commerce recently stated that American industry has no problem with its production. Its main problem is distribution. Effective salesmen are the key to distribution, and proper selection is the key to finding, using, and profiting from salesmen of good quality.

INDUSTRY MUST IMPROVE its ability to select top salesmen. Failure to date has stemmed from such errors as the belief that interest equals aptitude; the fakability of aptitude tests; the crippling emphasis on conformity rather than creativity; and the subdivision of a man into piecemeal traits, rather than understanding him as a whole person. Experience appears to be less important than a man's possession of the two central characteristics of empathy and ego drive, which he must have to permit him to sell successfully. Training can only succeed when the raw material is present.

Selecting men with empathy and ego drive should contribute in some degree to helping industry meet one of its most pressing problems: reducing the high cost of turnover and selecting genuinely better salesmen.

Note

1. Robert N. McMurry, "The Mystique of Super-Salesman-ship," HBR March–April 1961.

Originally published in 1964
Reprint R0607N

Low-Pressure Selling

EDWARD C. BURSK

Executive Summary

TRADITIONAL, high-pressure selling techniques were intended to talk the buyer into making a purchase—which often meant driving him to a decision rather than allowing him to reach it freely and independently. In this classic article from 1947, HBR editor Edward C. Bursk makes the case for replacing high-pressure selling with a milder approach, in which the salesperson does not so much "sell" the prospect as let him follow his natural inclinations to buy.

Bursk draws from his own business experience to support his points. He begins with a discussion of the advantages of low-pressure selling, the heart of which is the seller's sincerity. He then analyzes the reasons for the method's effectiveness. It's most clearly demonstrated by the customer-problem approach, in which the salesperson learns about the buyer's problems and, in effect, helps him solve them. Bursk concludes by addressing the practical questions facing sales managers, who bear the brunt of implementing the new technique. Low-pressure selling requires salespeople who are intelligent, analytical, subtle, and flexible—qualities rarely found in practitioners of the high-pressure selling method. Managers must not only craft a compensation plan that balances stability of income with strong incentives but select and train low-pressure salespeople with care.

SALES MANAGERS and salesmen in many lines decry "high pressure" selling as a crude relic of bygone days. More and more they are advocating what can only be described as "low-pressure" selling. Although the swing from high-pressure to low-pressure techniques was gathering momentum long before the war, the scarcities of the last few years have accelerated it. Now, at the end of the war and just before goods become plentiful again, it is imperative that we examine this shift in the thinking of those who have to do with selling, which has gone so far that viewed in retrospect it looks like a complete about-face.

What actually is low-pressure selling? Is it the absence of high pressure, whatever that may be, or merely high pressure in clever disguise? Why is it effective—because it is different and takes people by surprise (which means it may lose its power as time goes on and buyers become hardened to it), or because it taps basic human reactions? Is low-pressure selling sound and productive—enough so to keep moving the increased volume of goods that our postwar planning calls for? Or are sales managers and salesmen relying on spineless techniques that will fall flat in a real buyer's market?

It is the purpose of this article to try to answer these questions, and then to consider the implications for sales management. Attention will be confined to personal selling; that is, selling by salesmen, and specifically outside salesmen rather than retail salesmen in stores. It should not be forgotten, however, that there are obvious parallels in other types of promotional activity, and of course a company's personal selling strategy needs to be coordinated with its advertising program.

Furthermore, without wishing to anticipate the conclusions of this analysis, the author does want to acknowledge that he is chiefly concerned with selling to business buyers, both buyers for resale and industrial purchasers. These businessmen make buying decisions primarily on a rational rather than an emotional basis, and for this reason seem especially suited to low-pressure selling. There is no need, however, to rule out consumers. They too are now tending toward rational buying: Witness the growth of such organizations as Consumers' Research as well as the inauguration of high school instruction in buying as part of domestic science courses and the more realistic attitude of the younger generation in general. Even the brush salesman, who used to be considered the prime example of high-pressure selling, no longer finds it desirable to try to wedge his foot in the door; instead he draws back as the door is opened, smiles courteously at the housewife, hands her a sample brush (or booklet during wartime), and says he will call for the order tomorrow.

As a matter of fact, the overall trend toward more rational buying—hardheaded, discriminating, sophisticated—certainly has some connection with the trend toward low-pressure selling. Sales managers and salesmen have been alert to the change in buying attitudes, have capitalized on it in their selling techniques, and thus in turn have strongly reinforced it.

What Is Low-Pressure Selling?

Perhaps the easiest approach to deciding what low-pressure selling means is first to try to point out what it is not; that is, to define its opposite. Here we have as many definitions to choose from as there are people. Almost everyone who has ever bought anything nods his head when you say "high-pressure selling"; he has a feeling about it. Yet if all those feelings could be translated accurately into words, we might find them surprisingly uniform. Indeed, the factor that makes one kind of selling high-pressure and the other low-pressure may very well be the spirit in which the selling is done rather than anything more definite and concrete.

Some people will tell you, if you press them for a definition, that high-pressure selling means persuading the prospect to buy something that he cannot afford, that is not suited to his needs, that he does not want, and that will leave him dissatisfied after the salesman leaves. But that description, however characteristic, seems to denote the possible results of high-pressure selling rather than its fundamental meaning and purpose. Others call it "bludgeoning the prospect," "sweeping him off his feet," "not giving him time to catch his breath," "bewildering him," even "deceiving him." These phrases, although again they may be justified by the actions of many practitioners of high-pressure selling, seem more to suggest the manner in which such selling is sometimes performed than its fundamental nature.

Perhaps another phrase, "talking the prospect into buying," with the emphasis on "into," comes nearer to expressing what we want. For it simply implies that the prospect—or, by this time, the victim—has not reached the decision to buy through any rational, considered course of his own, but has been driven into it. This basic concept, that high-pressure selling means driving the prospect into a buying decision, fits in with and explains the other manifestations that we mentioned. Naturally, such selling can have the effect of leading a person to buy something not wanted (although it does not need to); and naturally it lends itself to what may be called "strong-arm" methods (although the element of trickery and deceit may be grafted on any kind of selling, including low-pressure selling).

With this concept of high-pressure selling in mind, we can now go on to define low-pressure selling. We want to beware of oversimplification. In actual practice, of course, low-pressure techniques overlap high-pressure techniques or show up in combination with them; what we usually see is merely a difference in the degree of selling pressure. For the purpose of analysis and clearer understanding, however, we need to think of low-pressure selling as something essentially separate and distinct, the veritable opposite of high-pressure selling; and this approach to it will be justified subsequently if our discussion indicates that it does have a meaning and purpose of its own.

LETTING THE PROSPECT DECIDE
FOR HIMSELF

Low-pressure selling, then, is not driving the prospect into a buying decision, but letting him reach the decision himself; not selling him, but letting him buy. Put this way, it sounds simple. But a closer examination immediately raises some serious questions that, unless they can be answered satisfactorily, cast doubt on the long-run desirability of low-pressure techniques.

The very fact that we defined low-pressure selling by saying that it was not high-pressure selling suggests that it is nothing more than a weakening of the degree of selling effort. Indeed, such a suspicion is not without a realistic basis, for there is actual danger that sales managers and salesmen, in turning from previous selling techniques, will not try to replace their obvious all-out effort—which enjoyed a substantial degree of effectiveness if only by reason of its aggressiveness—with positive methods of equal or greater effectiveness in the new area of low-pressure selling.

When we say that low-pressure selling means letting the prospect decide for himself, can we possibly mean that there is no attempt at all to influence him? If so, then the buying decision rests entirely on an examination of the relative merits of competing products (or of competing claims on the prospect's money, time, warehouse space, and so on). And if the advantages of the salesman's proposition are presented fairly, that is, accurately, then only the superior product will be bought. But this kind of selling, unless supplemented by positive action of some kind, would not be selling at all. It would be a sort of information service, which would be better handled by an impersonal and objective research organization. From the point of view of individual companies, it would be ineffective except in those rare cases of products with clearly demonstrable superiority. Clearly low-pressure selling has more positive character than that.

In the first place—and this touches directly on a fact that selling trainees find hard to appreciate—no matter how similar competing products may be in price and overall quality, each usually has at least one minor feature, either in the product itself or in the service and terms associated with the product, that is unique and that makes that product more desirable for certain purchasers than the other products. Consequently, the salesman can highlight his own product's particular advantage, still leaving it to the prospect to decide rationally among the advantages of competing products.

In the second place, some kinds of positive action can be employed. Let us continue to assume that the buyer is free to arrive at his decision principally through his own rational thought. Yet even without dramatic devices, fast talking, or any other features associated with the high-pressure approach, there will still be differences in the degree to which the salesman's presentation elicits attention and rouses interest, that is, differences in the effectiveness of selling techniques. Moreover, emotional appeals need not be eliminated entirely, although they must of course be introduced more subtly. In this connection, it may be pointed out that even in the case of large industrial buyers, presumed to be making decisions on a completely rational dollars-and cents basis, the appeal to vanity can often be employed without spoiling the effect of the low-pressure approach, and very tellingly. Consider, for example, the opportunity to stir up a feeling of pride in plant appearance when the attempt is being made to sell the president of a company a major item of equipment.

But how far can salesmen go in introducing appeals and other stratagems designed to put backbone in their low-pressure techniques and still be true to the idea of letting the prospect reach the buying decision himself?

NEED OF SINCERITY

There is the possibility, of course, that low-pressure selling can be used with the intention not so much of actually letting the prospect decide for himself as of making him think the decision is his own; in other words, trying just as hard to induce him to buy but disguising the attempt. Certainly, there is more than a shadow of truth in such a concept. It hardly seems realistic to suppose that the salesman should be any less eager to sell; let us hope that he is not, or the selling is likely to be completely ineffective. Why should not the salesman at least do his utmost to set a favorable environment for the prospect's decision? Here is plenty of opportunity for selling ability.

At the same time, we ought to doubt whether real low-pressure selling can be based on the out-and-out cynical concept that the salesman is tricking the prospect into buying by pretending that he is not trying to sell at all. This of course raises the question of ethics, which is a very vital question, worth much more thought than it usually receives from sales managers and salesmen. The ordinary way to meet it is to observe that a certain amount of, shall we say, "exaggeration" and "selection of facts" seems to be expected of salesmen, and any buyer who fails to take salesmen's statements and maneuvers with a few grains of salt is considered "fair game." But that is not enough of an answer.

Surely, the spirit that motivates a salesman is significant. Most enlightened sales managers and salesmen, not to mention buyers, would agree that there is a line, real but impossible to draw precisely, between legitimate and illegitimate use (or abuse) of exaggeration, half-truth, and other types of misstatement. On one side is the salesman's normal, expected display of enthusiasm for what he is selling, and on the other side is intention to deceive and mislead. Most enlightened sales managers and salesmen would also agree that the latter should be avoided, not only because it is bad ethics but also because it is bad business. In most lines of selling, and certainly in all lines of selling where reputation and prestige have any continuing value, the feeling is that such action sooner or later comes to light and loses more sales than it ever gained.

As a matter of fact, this disapproval of flagrant deceit—call it good ethics, call it good business, or call it a combination of the two—is an integral part of a definite evolution in the dignity of selling, from the wily peddlers of the past to modern "sales representatives" and "sales engineers." Moreover, it may well be that the trend toward low-pressure selling, considered in its "purest" form, is not so much the revolution that it seems to be as a part of the same long-run development.

In any event, it is clearly possible that low-pressure techniques will defeat their own purposes unless animated by a substantial degree of sincerity. Sooner or later, if buyers get "burned" by lowering their resistance in response to a pretense of fairness and candor, they will begin again to mistrust all sales presentations, and the field will be open to the "slam-bang" methods of yesterday. Furthermore, and entirely apart from the danger of reprisals in the future, there is serious doubt whether the technique can ever be made fully effective unless it actually is carried through with sincerity. There are several reasons for this: (1) It is never easy to keep deceit and insincerity from showing in one's talk and action; it is doubly hard when one is supposed to proceed calmly

and deliberately rather than in high-geared fashion.
(2) Sincerity is the very crux of low-pressure selling,
since the effectiveness of the technique hinges largely on
the salesman's appearance of concern for the prospect.
If a salesman is to convince a prospect by means of an
attitude, then the attitude must be given a convincing
demonstration, and that can hardly be done unless the
attitude is genuine.

With this understanding, then, do we still have any
right to say that trying to set a favorable environment for
the prospect's decision is compatible with being sincere
about letting the prospect decide for himself? But why
not? Concern for the prospect provides one of the most
effective ways to achieve the desired environment. Developed to its fullest form, such concern becomes what is
sometimes called "the customer-problem approach"; and
this approach, in turn, is the clearest crystallization of
low-pressure selling. Let us look at a specific example of
this approach and see how it works.

THE CUSTOMER-PROBLEM APPROACH

A company selling hosiery and underwear for men,
women, and children, principally to department stores,
found the customer-problem approach to be very hard to
inculcate in salesmen but very effective when the salesmen gave it a serious try. Although the company's products were of good quality and reasonable price, for each
item there was no demonstrable edge over the same
items in competitors' lines. However, the company did
have a unique feature to talk about: the fact that, because
of the unusually diverse line, quite a few different departments of a store could carry the company's brand, which
was backed by substantial national advertising.

The executives of the company realized that department stores faced a real problem in their choice between nationally advertised brands and private, or individual, store brands. The former offered the advantage of low customer resistance and quick turnover. The latter, on the other hand, made it possible for a store to realize on the reputation of a brand built up in one department by featuring it in some other department. For instance, a woman who had become convinced of the reliable quality of XYZ hosiery for herself would also be disposed to buy XYZ socks or underwear for her children when she came across them in those departments. The company's unusually diverse line seemed to offer the advantages of both horns of this dilemma, with few or none of the corresponding disadvantages.

In soliciting stores that had not previously been customers, the company's salesmen, like most salesmen, usually came up against the objection that the store already carried more brands of hosiery and underwear than it really should from the standpoint of inventory costs; and, since they all were good brands, well-recognized by consumers, it would only cut profits to add another brand. Such an objection is hard to dispose of, for it has a sound basis, and the salesmen were accustomed to try to dodge it or, when they could not do so, to try to overcome it by talking about the "superior" quality of their brand of products. At the same time, although the salesmen were very successful in holding old customers and increasing the sales volume of accounts already on the books, they were failing to add new customers as fast as the sales manager thought they should.

He therefore urged them to follow this approach: (1) to meet without flinching, or even to introduce

deliberately, the question of number of brands being
carried by the store, and to encourage the buyer to
talk about his problems in keeping inventory down;
then (2) to say in effect that the brands already carried
were of course good brands (thus flattering the buyer's
judgment), just as good indeed as the brand that the
salesman was offering; and finally (3) to point out that,
even so, the salesman's brand might help to solve the
store's problem because it combined the advantages of
national advertising and storewide reputation and thus
would make it possible for the store to realize more
sales, with a lower inventory cost per dollar of sales.

The plan worked. Note some of its points: There are
no exaggerated claims about the product's superiority; as
a matter of fact, the salesman compliments his competitors' brands. The salesman capitalizes on the one feature
that makes his line different from his competitors' lines.
There is a subtle appeal to the vanity of the prospect—
slight, to be sure, but all the more effective because it is
not obvious. The buyer is "opened up" by a question
about his problems, a subject dear to his heart and sure
to interest him; if it starts him talking, so much the better, for he is likely to give the salesman some good leads
for further sales points later in the presentation. And,
most important, by offering in effect to help him solve
his problems, the salesman has made the buyer feel that
he is making his own decision, and making it rationally.

This example should be enough to give a preliminary
idea of the way in which sincerity and purposeful effort
can be combined in low-pressure selling. Variations
will be brought in as illustrations as we go on to discuss the reasons for the apparent effectiveness of low-
pressure selling.

Reason for Effectiveness

It should be emphasized, to begin with, that low-pressure selling is not likely to be effective in equal degree in all kinds of selling and that it naturally needs to be modified to suit particular circumstances. Nevertheless, there appear to be certain basic reasons for its effectiveness.

THE ELEMENT OF THE UNEXPECTED

There seems little doubt that, at least in the earlier stages of their use, low-pressure techniques have been strengthened by the fact that prospects, expecting to be argued into buying, are taken aback and thrown off guard when exposed to a disingenuous approach. Take, for example, the story about the hardheaded businessman who was "poison" to experienced insurance salesmen, yet was "bowled over" completely by the fresh-faced lad who, admitting that he knew absolutely nothing about insurance, said such lack of knowledge didn't matter since the businessman in question was obviously the best judge of what size and kind of policy he ought to have. Of course it turned out to be a very large and expensive one.

There are obvious limitations to the usefulness of this factor. It hardly needs to be pointed out that if every insurance salesman intentionally tried the naive tactics referred to in the story, none of them would succeed. That fact again raises the question whether low-pressure techniques will continue to be effective as they become more and more common. Part of the answer lies in the observation that even now the prospect's surprise is not usually conscious or very extreme, and that in any event it must be supplemented by the salesman's use of

positive action. An ever larger part of the answer lies
in the soundness of the psychological aspect of low-
pressure techniques, which will be discussed in the next
section; in other words, there is a sounder basis for effectiveness than that provided by the contrast with an obvious all-out effort to sell. The brush salesman with his
new techniques may count on surprise the first time he
calls; yet on subsequent calls he continues to operate
with increased effectiveness.

At the same time, the element of the unexpected is
not to be disregarded entirely. There are many fields
where high-pressure techniques continue to be prevalent, and here the contrast provided by low-pressure
techniques undoubtedly adds some degree of strength
to the selling attempt. This is particularly true of what
may be called the "delayed-action approach" and the
"indirect approach," both of which lend themselves to
low-pressure selling.

EXAMPLE: DELAYED-ACTION APPROACH

The essence of the delayed-action approach is that
the obvious effort to secure a formal order is post-
poned beyond the normally expected time. Clearly, this
approach must be used with great care, lest salesmen,
too much inclined as it is to avoid coming to grips and
closing a sale, are further encouraged to shirk such
action out of laziness or timidity. The point must be
put across that despite the lengthening of time that
salesmen may spend on individual prospects, the purpose of the approach is to increase the number of
actual sales for the same expenditure of time and
effort, and this does demand decisive action in closing
sales at the proper moment. Clearly, too, this approach

cannot be used in all types of selling, particularly "one-shot" selling, where the sale must be made on the first call or not at all. Rather, it is best suited for building up a route of customers who will be called on regularly.

Perhaps an example will clarify the strategy of this approach—an example to which the author can testify personally, for it resulted from an experiment he made in opening a new territory for the wholesale grocery business that he at one time owned and operated. A group of approximately 30 retail stores were called on. Fifteen of them (every other one) were approached by the usual techniques, and orders were solicited from the very start. Five stores were sold on the first call, but several of these failed to repeat the second time, and ultimately only four of the 15 became regular customers. With the other 15 stores, however, absolutely no attempt was made to sell the first time; the call consisted only of a pleasant introductory explanation of why the company was expanding its territory, what it had to offer (specialized service rather than better price or better quality), and the remark that the salesman would call again next week. This call was followed up by a letter from the home office, thanking the storekeeper for his courtesy to the salesman and including two or three short sentences about company policy. Then the next week the salesman called again, this time asking for orders. Ten of the 15 stores placed orders, with all ten becoming regular customers.

This delayed-action approach was subsequently used to open other territories, with comparable results. Clearly, it was more productive to postpone trying to get orders beyond the first call, which was the normally expected time. Why? The element of the unexpected undoubtedly played some part: It surprised the prospects and had the effect of making them lower their guard. Also, something was gained by avoiding initial turndowns, for it is often harder to reverse turndowns than it is to get original orders. But probably most important was the simple fact that the approach avoided rousing unnecessary resistance in the prospects, and thus gave free play to the psychological factors discussed immediately below. The same comments could be made about the indirect approach, which will be illustrated subsequently.

PEOPLE LIKE TO BUY

This is the fundamental psychological reason for the effectiveness of low-pressure techniques. Assuming for the moment that none of the customary deterrents to buying are present, we can say that the act of buying gives the normal person a sense of pleasure. There is a certain feeling of power in being able to acquire things, entirely apart from any anticipation of enjoying the products or services bought. Buying flatters the ego. Certainly vanity is involved, particularly when a person thinks he is buying wisely and shrewdly, "getting a bargain." Incidentally, in this connection it is worth noting that in organizational shifts of function within business firms one of the powers least readily surrendered is the right to buy. There is also the happy fact that, unless impelled to the contrary, people like to be nice to other people; and if one of the other people happens to be a salesman, the way to be nice is to buy something. Finally, we have the gratification of desires and the anticipation of enjoyment in the case of consumer buying, and the expectation of profit in the case of business buying.

Most sales managers and salesmen do not appreciate the strength of this primary desire to buy. They are inclined to be obsessed by the fact that people do not seem to buy eagerly and without hesitation, and they are accustomed to thinking in terms of prodding people to buy, principally on the merits of the products and services that they sell. Consequently, they do not give enough attention to eliminating the deterrents and thus unleashing the buying urge.

As a matter of fact, there are many reasons why people ordinarily are not ready buyers. Consider, for example, such deterrents as doubt occasioned by conflicting claims on a prospect's limited money, time, interest, space; fear of being sold things not wanted or needed, based on past unfavorable experience with salesmen; caution and hesitation, springing from the desire to be sure of a good bargain; habit, that is, always buying certain products from certain sources—a much stronger deterrent than is usually realized; and so on. All these factors give occasion for "resistance," sometimes conscious but more often unconscious; and the composite result is that the prospect reacts adversely when he thinks he is being sold, being pushed into a decision. Conversely, therefore, to the extent that a prospect can be made to feel that he is reaching his own decision, the buying urge is free to express itself. It is this unleashing of the buying urge that gives such strength to the low-pressure techniques.

LULLING RESISTANCE

It should be recognized immediately that the word "resistance," although used in this article because it is a regular part of selling parlance and because there seems to be no suitable substitute, is too general to denote accurately what we mean by it; namely, the emotional state of mind—fear, doubt, caution, or whatever it may be—that in a particular sales situation keeps the prospect from buying as readily as he otherwise would. Excluded from our concept is any "holding off" due to a rational consideration of the wisdom of the purchase. Of course, this emotional state of mind may well be nurtured by actual unfavorable experiences with selling in the past, and it may well be prompted by wholly logical reasons that make it ill-advised or impractical for a prospect to make the specific purchase. Remember, too, that the prospect may tend to rationalize, expressing what are largely emotional reactions solely in terms of logical deterrents to the purchase ("I can't afford to buy"). Nevertheless, there is this, shall we say, disinclination to buy that is primarily emotional and that goes distinctly beyond reflecting the time and effort required to appraise a possible purchase rationally; and that is what we mean by "resistance" in this article.

Low-pressure selling gains effectiveness not only by virtue of the fact that it avoids rousing increased resistance in the way in which high-pressure selling does, but also because, if planned with care, it can exert positive action toward lulling whatever resistance is already present. In this connection, the delayed-action approach should be referred to again. Perhaps a more striking example is the way in which the indirect approach can be adapted to low-pressure selling.

EXAMPLE: INDIRECT APPROACH

There are many variations of the indirect approach, but the common characteristic is that the stage is set in such a way as not to stress the imminence of the selling attempt. The idea is that a strong head-on attack is likely to alarm the prospect and cause unnecessary resistance.

An extreme form of the indirect approach, with overtones reminiscent of high-pressure selling, is when the salesman calls in overalls, says he is sent to service a piece of equipment, finds something wrong (not necessarily honestly), and recommends a new purchase. Another variety, perhaps not so far over the borderline of good ethics, is the use of disguised and fancy titles, anything but plain "salesman," to conceal the salesman's business until the last possible moment. Such methods ("tricks" is a better word) are extremely questionable. They obviously cannot be used successfully in any kind of selling that depends on the development of goodwill over a period of time. Furthermore, they ignore one of the basic requisites of effective low-pressure selling: sincerity.

Such an approach, let it be emphasized, cannot have the purpose of trying to take advantage of the customer through a ruse if it is to be considered as genuine low-pressure selling. There should be no idea that the salesman is, so to speak, sneaking up on a prospect, deluding him into thinking that he is not being subjected to a selling attempt, and then getting him to say yes in a moment of false security. That is clearly the opposite of letting the prospect reach the buying decision principally through his own rational thought. Nor are such tactics necessary. There should be no reason to apologize for selling (that is, for the use of persuasion in the exchange of money for goods) either to society as a whole or to an individual prospect in a particular selling attempt. Applied wisely and with good motives, the indirect approach lulls resistance in the sense of decreasing the effect of what after all is largely an emotional attitude unrelated to the question of the merits of the particular purchase.

To be specific about the particular tricks just mentioned, it is the author's contention that, especially in dealing with businessmen, a salesman should divulge his real identity and mission at the very beginning of a sales interview. Such frankness will stand him in good stead. The prospect is difficult to fool, and he knows that his caller is not there just for pleasure or with the altruistic desire to help him somehow at no expense. So the frankness merely admits what the prospect probably already knows or suspects and capitalizes on it by showing that no pretenses are being made. Moreover, such a demonstration of matter-of-fact, straightforward dealing is not inconsistent with making the prospect feel he is reaching the buying decision himself. Indeed, it is more likely to be a positive help in that direction since it is in itself an unspoken argument that the salesman sees no reason for the prospect to show resistance.

Furthermore, and speaking more generally, there are plenty of maneuvers of an indirect type that are perfectly ethical and animated by sincerity—in other words, good examples of low-pressure selling. We can cite, again from the insurance field, the use of an offer to analyze the prospect's insurance needs or to "plan his estate." Many insurance companies do a very thorough and objective job in preparing such analyses, not hesitating to recommend types of insurance that they do not sell or even to approve of competing companies' policies that are similar to their own. If carried out sincerely, and that implies adequate knowledge and care, such an approach is extremely effective in lulling resistance—even though, of course, the prospect knows perfectly well that the ultimate aim of the salesman is to sell him insurance. The author remembers clearly, and still with a warm feeling after the lapse of a good many years, the occasion when an analysis of his "estate" was presented to him with the recommendation that he was carrying enough insurance at the time in relation to what he could afford financially. Needless to say, when subsequently he was in a better position to buy insurance, the salesman who had made the analysis got the business. (It should be noted that in this instance there is also an element of the delayed-action approach.)

Opening the interview by means of a question designed to start the prospect talking belongs in the same general category. It serves the purpose of securing attention and arousing interest; of putting the prospect at ease; and, if the salesman is adroit, of leading the conversation to a point where mention of the product being sold seems to come in almost automatically. A specific instance of this would be where a truck tire salesman, after introducing himself in his true colors, begins by asking the prospect if he has had much trouble with breakdowns along the road. But let it be emphasized: The salesman must be patient; he must have interest, and must be prepared to show interest, in the whole gamut of truck maintenance problems; his inquiry must be backed by both knowledge and sincerity; and he must depend on his own skill in developing the conversation to the proper point.

This particular example of using a question to lead indirectly to the purpose of a sales call and thus lull resistance is tied in with the customer-problem approach. The question technique can be used in other ways, and the customer-problem approach does not need to begin with a question or even to be carried through indirectly; yet the two sets of tactics work well together. Furthermore, as mentioned earlier, the customer-problem approach is the clearest crystallization of low-pressure selling. Because of its comprehensiveness and wholeheartedness, it is the most likely to make the prospect feel he is reaching the buying decision himself and thus requires mention in this discussion of the primary buying urge and how to unleash it for selling purposes.

FOCUSING ON THE OBJECTIVE RATHER THAN ON THE DETAILS

Particularly if we think of the customer-problem approach, we can see another reason for the effectiveness of low-pressure selling. Because it is based on sincere concern for the prospect, it leads him to the point of buying by setting up an objective toward which his mind moves naturally rather than by trying to work him through all the necessary mental stages one by one. The latter course depends on a degree of preciseness that is hard to achieve. Even if we could be sure that there was a definite sequence of mental reactions through which every prospect should pass as he decides to buy (more complicated, no doubt, than the traditional "attention, interest, desire, conviction"), and even if we knew just what they were, it would be hard to separate them in actual practice, harder to follow the prospect's course through them, and hardest of all to provide the proper stimulus for each of them at just the proper time.

Much sounder and much more fruitful than relying on any such "psychological" analysis of selling is the threefold process implied in the customer-problem approach: (1) What is the customer's need or want? (2) How does my product fit that need or want? (3) How can I best demonstrate the relationship between the two? Such a process has these distinct advantages: (1) It keeps the salesman's mind on one central purpose, yet allows adaptation to individual cases. (2) It suggests the motives that can best be appealed to in making a sale. (3) It does not arouse so much new resistance and may even lull resistance already present. (4) The completed sale leaves the customer satisfied.

In other words, low-pressure techniques gain added effectiveness because they are suited to the actual selling tasks of individual salesmen. In this connection, it should also be mentioned that the bugaboo of salesmen, closing the sale, may actually be easier with low-pressure techniques. To the extent that the prospect is made to feel that he is reaching the buying decision himself, and primarily through a rational process of thought, there is less need of extra push to establish "conviction" in his mind just before the salesman asks for the order. In the author's opinion, this matter of conviction is not generally understood. Being convinced is a state of mind that most buyers need to assume before giving the irretrievable yes to the salesman. It results from a final questioning and justification of the wisdom of the purchase, and as such it is primarily rational—at least more rational than the desire for the product, which may have been built up by the salesman largely on the basis of emotions. Therefore, in high-pressure selling with heavy emotional appeals there is likely to be something a little different and a little extra that must be added to the prospect's thinking at the next-to-last minute. In low-pressure selling, on the other hand, much of this last obstacle to the buying decision will often have been disposed of gradually as the sales presentation proceeds, and the prospect is already in the rational frame of mind to accept conviction—or even better, to convince himself.

SPECIAL CIRCUMSTANCES

Most of the observations made up to this point are applicable to low-pressure selling in general. From the various illustrations used, however, it should be evident that certain situations lend themselves better to such selling than do others. For the benefit of those who wish to consider specific selling jobs, let us try to draw together some of the determining factors. (1) Whenever continuing goodwill is at stake, as would be the case in building up a route where calls will be made with relative frequency, then the "friendliness" of low-pressure selling will be an aid. (2) Whenever specialized knowledge is of value to customers, such as technical help or market information, then the customer's feeling of confidence in the salesman and his company, engendered by low-pressure techniques, will facilitate sales. (3) Whenever the purchases involved are of more than ordinary significance to prospects, in dollars and cents or otherwise, then the feeling of having arrived at a well-considered decision will often be the affirmative factor. (4) Whenever the buyer intends to use the product or service for business purposes, such as resale for profit or use in industrial production, then the opportunity to apply rational judgment will reinforce the desirability of the purchase. The list does not pretend to be complete. Moreover, there are plenty of selling situations where, even without such special favoring circumstances, low-pressure selling will still outpull high-pressure techniques. After all, low-pressure selling owes its effectiveness to the fact that it is based on human nature.

What about the influence of different economic conditions on the effectiveness of low-pressure techniques? More specifically, are they likely to lose some of their strength in periods when buyers are balky? On the contrary, they should be stronger since then there is all the more need to lull the resistance of those who feel they must make their buying decisions with greater wariness and objectivity of judgment. All in all, the conclusion is justified that low-pressure selling has a tremendous potential of effectiveness—great enough, in the author's judgment, to provide the measure of difference between success and failure in our postwar plans for increased distribution of goods. Certainly low-pressure selling, particularly in the form of the customer-problem approach, is pointed in the right direction, toward the satisfaction of the economic needs and wants of ultimate consumers, which from the point of view of society is the only long-run justifiable end of both production and distribution. Furthermore, while like all selling effort it involves expenditure of money to persuade people to buy (the inevitable counterpart of purchasers' freedom to buy when, where, and what they will), this particular type of selling does add validity to the idea that the costs of distribution that society bears, although not showing up as tangible values in products, are justified by intangible services rendered to the economy; and at the same time, it may help to reduce these costs through its greater effectiveness.

Whether its potential can be realized, however, depends on whether sales managers are willing to tackle the increased problems of selection and training of salesmen.

Implications for Sales Management

It was mentioned earlier that low-pressure selling runs the danger of being ineffectual unless the absence of high pressure is compensated for by positive effort. It should be clear by now that more is required of salesmen using this technique than merely being pleasant— although it is important here, certainly more important than in high-pressure selling, that the salesmen's personal habits and manners create a favorable impression with prospects, since so much is staked on not arousing resistance. It should also be clear by now that more is required of salesmen than a series of soft and subtle little stratagems to replace their old exaggerated claims and emotional appeals; they must utilize something strong and purposeful, like the customer-problem approach.

All this puts a heavy burden on sales management in the selection and training of salesmen. This task is both more important and more difficult with low-pressure selling. Low-pressure selling may have some of the powers of the magic lamp, but it takes a good deal of hard rubbing to produce the jinni. For the purpose of this article it will have to suffice to mention the management problems raised by low-pressure selling and to indicate the general direction in which solutions must be sought. As a matter of fact, the nature of low-pressure selling is so flexible that most specific problems have to be handled in terms of individual companies.

SELECTION OF SALESMEN

A different type of salesman is needed. No attempt can be made here to specify his qualifications since there are so many factors to be weighed and taken into account in individual selling jobs, but the general outline indicates a decided departure from the hail-fellow-well-met, back-slapping, storytelling, loud-laughing type of the traveling salesman and farmer's daughter era. Indeed, many sales managers have already found that the ambivert or even the near-introvert is likely to be more successful than the extrovert.

Above all, a more intelligent type is needed for low-pressure selling. A normal man will not find it unnatural or difficult to assume the habit of thinking in terms of his customers' problems, but he will have to do a greater amount of more subtle thinking—adapting to individual cases and swinging sales on finer points. Certainly he cannot operate by rote and ritual.

Clearly, it will take more care and effort to select such men. There is no point here in going into the controversial subject of how prospective employees can best be appraised, but it will do no harm to point out that in this case the qualities sought may not be readily apparent, and that a well-planned system of detailed application forms, multiple interviews, and psychological testing seems indispensable.

TRAINING OF SALESMEN

It is relatively easy to teach high-pressure techniques. Because the essence of that approach is that the prospect submits to something imposed on him from without, it is possible to standardize the sales presentation—to formulate it in the home office and show the salesmen how to do it. The opposite is the case with low-pressure selling. Although of course something can be prepared in the way of suggested openings, possible answers to objections, and so on, any hint of a "canned" sales talk, learned and repeated from memory, will ruin a low-pressure approach completely.

Two principal duties devolve on the sales manager who would have his salesmen do effective low-pressure selling. In the first place, he must give them knowledge about the company's products and policies and about the customers' needs and ways of doing business. He must give them everything he can think of and then encourage them to come back at him with questions and requests for additional information. Such knowledge will give a feeling of confidence to the salesmen—and to the prospect too, when he sees it in evidence. Such knowledge is indispensable for low-pressure selling in general and the customer-problem approach in particular.

In the second place, the sales manager must train his salesmen to think—to think about their customers' individual needs and wants and how the company's products can fit those needs and wants. This is no easy task. How can it be accomplished? The author knows of no way that has ever been successful in training the ordinary run of human beings to think except by making them practice it in group discussions. For our present purpose, this would mean analyzing and arguing example after example of pertinent problems, preferably drawn from the actual experiences of salesmen in the field. Perhaps some of the new developments in visual education will be helpful in this connection, particularly the use of specially made movie shorts. There is no surer way of putting problems across than to present them in a form as close as possible to that in which they actually occur, and the greater vividness and realism thereby secured will stimulate the ensuing thinking and discussion.

LEADERSHIP

There is the further question of how salesmen can be controlled and directed in the field so that they will make the best use of low-pressure techniques. Several areas for possible action suggest themselves. Salesmen's reports can be used with this end in view; perhaps one report should be designed with no other purpose than to highlight the importance that management attaches to results other than immediate sales. Some of the sales meetings can be devoted exclusively to analysis of customers' needs. In this and other ways, relations between salesmen and their supervisors can be made more direct and intimate.

Certainly, too, there must be a logical tie-in with the plan for compensating salesmen. Of course, no sales manager can expect that he will ever have a perfect compensation plan, since inevitably it will be a compromise between objectives that are by nature contradictory. With low-pressure selling it is especially difficult to strike a balance between (1) stability and assurance of income, characteristic of straight salary, which make it easier for a salesman to engage in action not necessarily productive of immediate sales and to plan on the course that will bring in more sales and sounder sales in the long run, and (2) strong incentives, like commissions, which are useful in keeping a salesman at the peak of his effort yet may encourage him in a tendency to think only in terms of quick sales. Obviously, with low-pressure selling there is both more need of developing the long-run view and more danger of encouraging relaxation of effort; both objectives of the compensation plan become more important! However, in general it can be said that the logic of low-pressure selling points away from any emphasis on automatic incentive features—and indicates a bigger role for the sales manager, who must use other means to keep each salesman working to the best of his ability.

Above all, the sales manager must take extraordinary precautions to avoid some of the dangerous situations that might otherwise arise in connection with low-pressure techniques. He must make sure that the salesman, put more on his own and deprived of standardized props, does not flounder. He must make sure that the salesman does not "go with the wind"—hoping sales will develop rather than planning and working for them. He must make sure that the salesman does not take refuge by going over so completely to the customer's point of view that he neglects his primary function of selling the company's products.

To carry through this difficult assignment requires leadership and exercise of teaching ability. For it is harder to "drive" salesmen when the selling activity itself seems to have a slower tempo, and no automatic devices can do the trick.

Yet if the sales manager can succeed in educating his salesmen, and continually reeducating them, to the fact that low-pressure selling does demand as much positive, purposeful, planned action as high-pressure selling—and indeed more, in the sense that it must be deployed with greater skill and must have more effect for the same amount of obvious exertion—then low-pressure selling will actually bring higher productivity in relation to the time and effort spent. Furthermore, because the field is difficult, the rewards for superiority will be greater.

As mentioned before, the burden on sales management is heavy. But it is a burden that will reward those who take it up, for low-pressure selling, wisely used, can be the tool to increase sales. And let it not be forgotten that management has the clear responsibility of seeing that effective selling does accelerate the distribution of goods—with personal selling, judged by the portion of the sales dollar that goes to it, still the most important aspect of distribution. If that responsibility is shirked, not only will individual companies fall behind in the bitter competitive struggle that probably lies ahead, but the whole country's hope for a more productive economy will end in disillusion.

T HERE IS LITTLE that the author cares to add at this point. He would like, however, to cover himself for some of the exaggerated statements and overdrawn distinctions he has made. Nothing is quite so black or white as he often has tried to make it look. For example, he has failed to say explicitly that there are bound to be selling situations where a judicious admixture of high-pressure techniques can be employed effectively and without harm to either the customers or the salesman's company. Even worse, he has talked as if most selling were soliciting new customers, whereas actually the bulk of selling activity consists of calling on old customers. Nevertheless, here too most of the observations made in the article apply, since the task of keeping old customers in line and increasing the size of their orders is still selling. As a matter of fact, it is this field that lends itself best to low-pressure selling, and it is here that many of the low-pressure techniques originated many years ago.

A further note of humility is also in place, on behalf of all salesmen as well as the author. One should never be dogmatic about selling. It is too closely related to the bewildering variousness of human nature—and this, again, is one of the reasons why low-pressure selling, with its flexibility and adaptability, is both more effective and more fun. What more appropriate conclusion to this article could there be, then, than the following story, which has always struck the author as a perfect illustration of (1) why never to be sure about what will happen in selling and (2) the dangers of not using the customer-problem approach? Let him tell it in the first person, since he played the central, if not heroic, role:

I had bought a carload of peas from a well-known canner that were slightly substandard—in other words, a little wrinkled and tough—and that the canner was not willing to pack under his regular brand. At that time, nationally advertised brands of peas were selling at about $2.25 a case; unadvertised but reasonably good brands were selling at $1.95. I had bought these peas so that, if I could turn them over fast, a price of $1.60 a case was satisfactory. I had a customer out in the country, a successful grocer accustomed to buying in large quantities, who I thought might be a good prospect. After figuring out how I could best approach him and deciding to stake everything on the price appeal, I got in my car and went out to call on him.

When I came into his store, I left the sample can of peas that I had brought with me in the car. As soon as he was free, I started to work with a price of $1.90 (thinking to myself that anything I could get above $1.60 would be "gravy"). Of course, the first question he asked me was, "Where is your sample?" So rather reluctantly, protesting that the name of the canner should be enough for him, I went out to my car to get it. We opened the can; he tasted a few, rolling them around in his mouth in a sort of judicious way, then chewing them rather deliberately. I said, "Pretty good, aren't they?" He countered, "Sort of tough, aren't they?" I said, "Well, not really; and at that price they are a bargain"—or words to that effect. After almost an hour of haggling, we had reached the point where he wouldn't go any higher than $1.60 and I wouldn't go any lower than $1.65. So I sold the carload to him at $1.625 a case—a whole 2.5 cents above the minimum price I had set myself.

And I felt pretty good about my sale. That is, I felt pretty good until he turned toward me, and smiled, and said, "You know, you made a bad mistake. I would have been glad to pay a premium for those peas instead of getting them for a bargain. I have been looking for peas exactly like that for a long time. The farmers that live around here like to cook their peas for a couple of hours, and most of the canned peas you get these days fall apart if you cook them that long."

Originally published in 1947
Reprint R0607M

Making the Major Sale

BENSON P. SHAPIRO AND RONALD S. POSNER

Executive Summary

MANY COMPANIES TODAY are faced with large, complex selling situations—they sell expensive equipment that affects many parts of a customer's company, they work on sales that may take several years to consummate, or they arrange mergers with other organizations. These major sales need special handling: They are more complex than smaller transactions, their potential profit is larger, and they have a more lasting effect on both buyer and seller.

In this article, first published in 1976, the authors develop a systematic approach that companies can use not only to facilitate the sale but also to ensure the long-term account relationship. Their eight-step procedure shows how to open a contact, "separate the suspects from the prospects," develop a profile of a company's needs and key personnel, justify the purchase to the buyer, make the sales pitch, coordinate company resources, close the sale, and maintain the account.

Before they can engage in strategic selling, most companies will have to revise the makeup of their sales forces according to the kind of sales they want to make, which may include different types of nonrecurring sales. To help solve these more-complicated selling problems, the authors provide organizational guidelines for companies to use in their specific operations. Among these are creating a senior sales force to service a multitude of major accounts, assigning a field sales manager to one or two accounts for regional sales management, and having top executives take charge of the large sales.

It has become increasingly clear over the past 15 years that salesmanship has been changing, especially when one business sells industrial or consumer goods and services to another.[1] As a result, the salesperson is being called on to perform in a different way.

One major change is that as mergers and acquisitions, sales of parts of companies, and different kinds of corporate financing have become more prevalent, the one-of-a-kind, nonrepetitive sale—such as the sale of a subsidiary or company, or a licensing arrangement—has become more important. These transactions have always existed, but they are more numerous and significant now and are beginning to attract the attention of sales management.

Second, businesses have become larger (and at the same time more complex), and the average size of the sale has grown. In certain industries, this change has been dramatic, especially with the development of system selling and large private-label contracts in consumer goods. Consider these examples:

- The Industrial Chemical division at Allied Chemical has sold sulfuric acid for many years. Its larger annual contract sales have been in the $1 million to $2 million range and have lasted for several years. Recently, the division developed a process for air pollution control whose sales involve a total capital commitment for a utility of more than $20 million and cover many years.

- Private-label contracts for consumer goods have not only grown in size but have also gone beyond the traditional general merchandise chains (Sears, Roebuck; J. C. Penney; and Montgomery Ward) to cover supermarkets, discount department stores, and regular department stores. Arrangements involving more than $10 million are not uncommon with such contracts.

- Even comparatively small companies are making large sales. In the field of building cleaning and maintenance, companies with $10 million in sales often compete for million-dollar contracts.

- The outcome of a few large sales can sometimes determine a company's well-being.

For example, one of Lockheed's major continuing problems has been low sales of the L1011 aircraft.

In industry, the consequences of the repetitive sale are often even more profound than the initial commitment itself; for system selling, one purchase decision can involve capital, supplies, raw material, and processes. The sale of a computer system can seriously affect a corporation's procedures and policies for many years. Methods of financial reporting, inventory control, production control, marketing, and administration can all be affected.

As the complexity of the purchase and the risk involved have increased, so have the cost and intricacy of selling and servicing the account. The average industrial sales call costs more than $70, with some sales requiring years to consummate. Larger sales often require special products and services and even custom manufacture. For example, most private-label lines are designed expressly for one customer.

Because the major sale affects many functional departments of the buyer, decision making is becoming more involved and the buying criteria more sophisticated. Naturally, the buyer's personnel are concerned over such a large purchase and must carefully evaluate its impact on their operations. Thus they need continuing reassurance and, in particular, more financial data—data such as return on investment and cost/performance measurements.

In this article, we will try to develop a program of responses that marketers can use in confronting these two new situations. After explaining the basic approach, we unfold eight steps management should take to ensure a more successful and long-lasting sale. Finally, we provide some organizational guidelines to help companies incorporate this approach into their overall activities.

The Basic Approach

Major sales, including both onetime sales and continuing relationships, need special handling: They are more complex, their potential profit is larger, and they have a more lasting effect on both buyer and seller. A systematic approach that works for both types of selling situations is strategic selling. This is a meticulously planned, total process, requiring coordination of the buyer and seller, that identifies the customer's needs and relates the company's products to those needs.

Strategic selling is especially relevant for "big-ticket" sales because only large potential profit can justify the careful planning and large amounts of resources that are required. Although it is not a new technique, it is attracting attention because it brings to bear more people, greater resources, and more information about the customer's needs; these characteristics uniquely suit the changes that have taken place in salesmanship.

The process is particularly effective because it emphasizes the dual goals of making the sale and developing account relationships. With escalating profits and longevity of sales, this latter goal is increasingly important. In fact, for repetitive major sales the objective should be to develop long-term account relationships, not just sales. The supplier with an established account relationship has a significant competitive advantage. Because risks are high and an intimate buyer/seller relationship builds up over time, buyers are hesitant to try new suppliers and tend to remain with established ones (unless the relationship becomes unbearable or costs increase significantly).

In fact, several corporations believe that their best prospects are current customers. For example, experts in the computer industry claim IBM statistics show that each new account's purchases grow eight times in every six years—this means that the new $5,000-per-month account will be producing $40,000 per month in six years.

Since satisfactory account relationships are an advantage to a marketer, the salesperson has two responsibilities: (1) to stress the long-term benefits of the account relationship to the customer and (2) to help develop trust and credibility in himself and his company.

There is a definite trade-off between "forcing" a customer to buy something and developing a long-term relationship with that customer. This trade-off can lead to a phenomenon called the "Pyrrhic sale," in which the sale is made at the expense of the account. In long-term relationships the customer is repeatedly in the position of being able to purchase the product. This circumstance requires the salesperson to manage the account carefully: If he (or she) forces a marginal sale, this often destroys credibility and the opportunity for future sales. But if the salesperson is willing to forgo a sale that is not in the long-term interest of the account, he can build his relationship with that account.

For example, the seller of apparel who is willing to tell a customer that some items in his line do not sell well at retail, in spite of their apparent appeal, helps his customer and himself over the long run. Or picture the response a buyer would give to the pump salesperson who says, "Yes, we offer the best pumps for your needs *a, b,* and *c,* but unfortunately, our pumps are not as good for application *d* as those offered by competitors *x* and *y.*"

The onetime sale is a somewhat different situation, in that the buying company is even more careful in protecting its interest. But the seller should still want to "leave a good taste in the buyer's mouth" because the sale is visible in the business community, especially within the particular industry, and because the buyer and seller will often be involved with each other after the sale. For example, the managers of a company being acquired often become employees of the buying company. Thus they want to structure a sale that will leave all parties satisfied. This is also true of licensing arrangements and other onetime sales that create lasting relationships.

One of the intriguing aspects of the onetime sale is that both sides are usually selling to each other. For example, the acquiring company often spends a great deal of effort selling the managers of the potential acquisition on the benefits of the merger. This leads to a two-sided romance negotiation in which both parties are sellers and buyers. Thus strategic selling can be applied not only to both types of major sale but also to both sides of the onetime sale.

Step by Step

Strategic selling is an eight-part process that develops the sale from the initial decision to pursue a prospect, through the appropriate strategy for courting an account, to the eventual close of the sale. Because strategic selling is also concerned with developing account relationships, the process is not complete without a discussion of how to sustain those relationships. Let us take a look at each of these steps in turn.

1. OPENING THE SELLING PROCESS

In preparing for a sale, the salesperson should do enough homework so that he has an idea of the likelihood of a sale and the appropriate person to contact initially. Assuming he feels he has a chance to make the sale, his next step is to make the "opening," which is often done over the telephone. His object is to gain

enough information from the initial contact to determine the most appropriate person or people to meet.

The best opening, particularly for onetime sales, is
sometimes made through a third party; this enables the
seller to gain recognition and credibility, avoid making a
cold call that puts him at a disadvantage, and obtain
information without announcing his intentions. Some
companies have developed proven third parties into a
"second sales force." Consider these examples:

- A young Los Angeles–based company that sells television production services always finds it easier and
more effective for its duplication and distribution
supplier to make the introduction. The latter company has been in business 30 years and has established an excellent reputation and a large, satisfied
customer base.

- Bank of America is training its corporate loan officers
to approach CPAs for an introduction to the latter's
clients.

For these third-party openings and references to work
over a period of time, both parties have to get something
from the arrangement. Frequently, such informal relationships work out so well for each party that a more formal sales agreement results in a commission or royalty to
the third party for introductions that lead to firm orders.

2. QUALIFYING THE PROSPECT

The next step is to determine whether a sale can eventually be made, or as someone has described it, to
"separate the suspects from the prospects." Unfortunately, many companies appear to spend more time

selling to prospects who have no intention of buying than to those who do. The old criterion of numbers—which measured selling effectiveness by the number of sales calls—is no longer valid; what matters is the quality of the call. The salesperson should ask himself questions like these:

- Does this prospective buyer really have a need for my product?

- Do the top managers recognize that need?

- If they don't, is it likely that I can educate them?

- Can I justify my product as a response to that need?

- Can I identify influential buyers and others who may affect the decision to buy?

All of these questions boil down to two equally important issues: (1) Can my company be of service to their company? and (2) Can I bring the two companies together? It's almost impossible, for example, for a salesperson to compete with another eager seller who has a close relationship, such as a family tie, with the prospective buyer.

Psychologically, the qualification process is difficult for a salesperson to accept because he has historically been taught that the "lead" is his most valuable possession. What he must learn now is that if the lead is not likely to become a sale, he should not pursue it, and that he is going to have to make the decision about its potential for himself. Not only does he have to ask penetrating questions like those mentioned previously, but he might also have to break off a friendly relationship if it doesn't promise any business.

3. DEVELOPING THE SALES STRATEGY

In strategic selling, so many activities are required, so much information has to be obtained, and so many influential people have to be attended to that it is easy to overlook important considerations.

Once he thinks the sale is possible, the salesperson needs a plan to enable him to direct his own efforts and to deploy his company's resources to make the sale and develop the account relationship. What we call the "Strategic Sales Opportunity Profile" is a simple technique to help him map out his entire strategy and organize his sales effort so that all the bases have been covered.

On one form, the salesperson can list people contacted, information obtained, his own activities, follow-up action, and results of the contact. The information he obtains will vary widely, from the practical (certain individuals need detailed cost estimates, or specific product and application data) and organizational (they will only negotiate with the seller's organizational counterpart or need reassurance about their role vis-à-vis the purchase), to the personal (they prefer concepts to details or cannot make a decision unless one of their associates confirms it).

If he completes the profile carefully, updates it regularly, and pursues each selling activity to its conclusion, he will be more likely to close the order. In addition, if he loses a sale, he will be able to make a better postmortem diagnosis.

The profile can also provide valuable information to product and market planning personnel at headquarters. By accumulating the data from the profiles nationally, planners can see trends, such as new applications for their current products, and the need for new products or services.

The salesperson's strategy should be based on the detailed information he has gathered during and after his analysis of the buyer. If he has grasped the idea of strategic selling, he will have asked the right questions: Will the person I'm going to call on make the actual decision? What kind of person is he? How does he fit into the organization? What is his background? Is it technical? Managerial? Where did he work before?

His strategy should also ensure that all of the influential buyers receive attention and the appropriate kind of attention (for example the traditional lunch or dinner, or financial data for the treasurer, or technical information for the engineering manager).

The key to strategic selling is calling "high and broad," something most salespeople fear or don't understand. They can talk to a purchasing agent or plant supervisor with relative impunity, but the prospect of calling on a president or an executive vice president frightens them. Although they know that high-priced sales decisions are made at very high levels, they often sell only at the lower levels, where they feel more comfortable, and let the middle-management contacts they have made there carry the story to top management.

This decision has two detrimental effects: (1) Some of the strength of their sales presentation is lost in the transmittal, and (2) what is even more damaging, the salesperson often loses a chance to develop a relationship with top managers and to directly gather data on the situation as these managers perceive it. After all, top managers are the people most affected by major purchases, since they will probably have to alter corporate policies and procedures to accommodate the new product or service.

For example, the salesman for a materials handling system spent three months with the director of western warehouse operations of a large New York–based manufacturing company. All along, this contact assured the salesman that he made all the decisions for his area. Unfortunately, competition got the business for the four *regional* warehouses because it won over the VP of operations in New York, who had the budget approval for all new warehouse systems.

4. ORGANIZING THE JUSTIFICATION

Once the salesperson has determined whom to contact (and at a high enough level), it is time to assist the company in cost-justifying the purchase. For the company to make a decision on a multimillion dollar product or service, each top executive will have to understand exactly how the purchase will affect *his* operation, budget, cash flow, and personal concerns.

So, at this stage of the strategic sales process, the salesperson must meet with each top executive affected by the purchase to determine his position, unique needs, and the qualitative and financial criteria he uses to justify large purchases. This entails becoming completely conversant with the prospect's operations, gaining a detailed grasp of its finances, and understanding the effect the seller's products and services will have on those operations. In effect, the salesperson should know as much as or even more about such matters than do some of the prospect's top people.

The salesperson is more likely to succeed if he understands the few really important variables that will eventually affect the final sale. Then he can limit the data he needs to those pieces of information and the sources for that information.

Since most cost justifications will be based on certain key assumptions, it is important to get a consensus on each assumption from the decision makers. Even when the salesperson isn't sure how the purchase will affect the organization, he can solicit opinions on potential cost benefits. Answers to such questions as, "Do you feel our service can increase sales by 10% over a two-year period?" or "Have you achieved a 5% decrease in labor costs with similar machinery in the past?" from several top executives can give the salesperson a way to justify the purchase, or at least to test alternative solutions to the prospect's problems. The object is to focus on what the prospect thinks is feasible and to use *his* numbers, not those the selling company believes are possible. By combining the best points made by each manager, the salesperson stands a better chance of having his reasoning accepted by the purchaser.

If he gathers data correctly, the salesperson will discover that this is his best time to sell; the decision makers are most free during this phase to say, "Here's what I want" and "Here's how I want to be sold."

5. MAKING THE PRESENTATION

The presentation summarizes all of the relevant information in the form of a proposal. If the right people are in attendance, the salesperson should usually use the presentation as an opportunity to ask for the order. While there is no established pattern for the most effective sales presentation, the selling company should carefully consider these factors: elements and order of presentation, location, timing, and who will be listening.

Elements and order of presentation. The best selling presentations deliver no new information to the audience. The presentation should only summarize the agreements previously reached with each of the decision makers, thus reinforcing the agreed-on solutions, cost justification, and the implementation commitments. People used to working with committees will be familiar with this approach: A typical way to handle a committee is to personally sell each committee member on a proposal before the meeting and then to gather general agreement at the meeting.

The sidebar "Elements of a Formal Presentation" at the end of this article shows the elements that a selling company should consider for a formal presentation. Note that the presentation basically flows from action to analysis to implementation. The summary is listed first because it outlines the conclusions and recommendations of the study, and because it provides the audience with a general understanding of the direction of the proposal.

Location. Marketing and sales managers often neglect the many possibilities open to them for a location—such as the prospect's facilities, a rented hotel or conference center space, the selling company's own seminar or presentation facility, an installation done for another customer, or a mobile display unit mounted in a trailer or bus.

Timing. This is another element that will be critical to the effectiveness of a presentation. If a salesperson and the prospect haven't reached mutual agreement on major points, such as the seller's analysis, then the presentation may be premature.

Attendees. The selling company should make sure that all decision makers are at the meeting, and invite those people within its organization who can best represent it from a social as well as business point of view—in other words, the counterparts of the prospect's personnel. The total group should be small enough to remain intimate and workable. The seller should also ensure that the presentation has enough variety of speakers to be interesting but not confusing. Some team members may take active roles, some may provide supportive information, and others may be there primarily as a formality.

For several reasons, the personal involvement of top managers is justified, and frequently required, by the buying company. First, they are the only people who can make the commitments the buyer requires—that is, adjust the selling conditions (including price, delivery, product features, and quality) and make and guarantee commitments that would sound hollow coming from lower management.

Second, they have the appropriate status to deal with top executives in the buying organization, who feel more comfortable dealing with their organizational counterparts.

Third, strategic selling involves more risk and requires greater resources—including higher-powered salespeople and better developed programs and sales aids—than the more typical approach. Only top managers can provide the discipline, allocate the resources, and establish the high standards such a program needs. Moreover, they have to provide continual motivation to a sales force that can easily become discouraged by a long lead time for sales. Their interest and involvement can be demonstrated not only by attendance at the presentation but also by account reviews with the sales representative and direct sales calls on the prospective buyer. (For the non-repetitive sale, their involvement is perhaps more crucial—only they can abrogate standard policies and procedures to provide the attention and resources needed on a onetime basis.)

6. COORDINATING RESOURCES AND PERSONNEL

During the selling process, the salesperson is responsible for managing the resources of his company, which may include financial, operations, nonsales marketing, and general management personnel and resources. For example, a private-label sale might involve a special product configuration (product development and design personnel), production capacity (manufacturing), warehousing and delivery requirements (distribution), and special costs, pricing, and payment schedules (finance and control). In addition, because the salesperson makes the major decisions and commitments, he should thoroughly understand his company's organizational, operational, and cost structure. For example, he must know what effect the commitment to deliver a large amount of a particular product will have on the company's ability to operate profitably. He should also understand the other functional areas of his company and be able to work with the personnel.

An interesting by-product of the salesperson's introduction of other resources into the prospect company is
the new lines of communication that are developed
between the seller and the buyer. If they are introduced
and coordinated effectively, these new resources can
assist the salesperson in building the account relationship after the order is signed.

The salesperson must be given a good deal of freedom
to make decisions about the sale. If a large prospective
customer is interested in a minor product modification, he must be able to respond quickly to that need—
either positively or negatively. If the buyer gets a run
around such as, "Let me check with my boss so that he
can check with engineering and manufacturing," the sale
will be lost.

Marketing as a primary resource. In the marketing
department alone, the salesperson may need to call on
product, pricing, and advertising support, as well as sales
promotion and sales aids. Many major accounts need
special products or modification of existing products
(such as private labels, packaging, and product-related
servicing), and their volume often makes such cus-
tomization justifiable. For example, a large fastener company packages its general-line fasteners in special con-
tainers for large users. The customer can feed highly
mechanized equipment automatically by using the packing container as a feed bin.

Because of their volume, major accounts often desire
substantial price concessions. Although the Robinson-
Patman Act puts limits on both requests and grants for
special concessions, some can be cost justified. In many
situations, a buyer does not contest the price itself so
much as the net cost of the acquired goods and services.

To the buyer, special delivery patterns, payment patterns, and other concessions are sometimes more important than the price per se.

Occasionally, major accounts are especially interested in customer-designed advertising or sales promotion programs. For example, large retailers with many stores sometimes find manufacturers who provide heavy in-store support particularly attractive. Such suppliers are often more responsive to the desires of the retailer's merchandising manager than are his own store managers. Thus the in-store support is worth more to the retailer than it costs the supplier.

However, all extra services cost money. Because they are more expensive and more unusual than in ordinary sales, the selling company must carefully analyze their cost and sales impact.

7. CLOSING THE SALE

Because of the complexity of the selling process and the length of the selling cycle, the close is the first concrete evidence that the salesperson is successful. Since the signature may occur anywhere from six months to three years after the start of the sales process, the salesperson should close on each "call"—that is, he should get an agreement from the prospect up to that point in the sales cycle. Since changes in the sales situation—such as a change in decision makers, or a shift in competitive strategy—can take place between calls, it is also a good idea to reaffirm or close again on previous agreements reached on each call.

By continually asking and getting answers to such questions as, "If we could deliver that system with an average ROI of 15% per annum, would you buy?" the salesperson knows well before the process is completed whether he has won the sale. If many decision makers give him negative responses, he can get out before too much time and money have been invested.

8. NURTURING THE ACCOUNT RELATIONSHIP

Some top marketers feel that the real selling starts after the order is signed for a major sale. For instance, a manufacturer of complex process control systems who performed a profitability analysis of each account discovered that 25% were unprofitable because of poor account management and salesmanship after the order had been signed.

If the product requires installation, training of personnel, or extended delivery schedules, the chances of the sale going sour increase unless the salesperson effectively controls the account. One way for him to do this is to develop a long-term plan for his products, services, and resources with the customer. He should also have his own account plan (like the Strategic Sales Opportunity Profile), which repeats most of the previous eight steps in qualifying, justifying, and developing strategies to expand the account. (His plan would be a more complete version of the plan he develops with his client.) For this planning process to work, he must involve the customer with the plan. In addition, the salesperson must locate inside advocates early to multiply his efforts in the account when he is not there.

The most important thing the salesperson can do is to keep selling contacts on the correctness of their buying decision, so that "buyers' blues" don't set in. He should continue as liaison between his company and his customer throughout delivery, installation, and usage. By dovetailing his product or service with his customer's operations and by making sure the product is producing the promised returns with the best utilization, the salesperson provides the extra assurance of add-on orders for his company and profitability for the customer. Postsales service not only reinforces the customer's confidence in the seller but also tends to keep competition out, since the customer's people are too busy working with the seller.

Organizational Guidelines

Because the strategic selling process is considerably more complex than the typical sales process, it requires new organizational techniques. For a company to solve more involved selling problems, it will have to revise the makeup of its sales force, depending on the kind of sale it wants to make; it must find solutions not only for recurring and non-recurring sales but also for different *kinds* of recurring sales.

VARIATIONS ON A THEME

A company can handle the repetitive major sale in several ways. Where strategic selling is necessary throughout the sales organization (for example, when selling computers, heavy equipment, or private-label food packers) management can concentrate on developing that strategy alone. However, many companies do not use strategic selling alone. In that situation, management may find it useful to separate strategic selling from other types of selling and use one of the approaches that follow.

Special sales force. When a company has many major accounts and prospects, typical in the food and packaged-goods industries, it can use a special sales force of senior sales representatives to service them. Most food manufacturers and the larger food brokers assign their major salespeople to cover the buying offices of the large food chains and wholesalers, while assigning junior salespeople to the individual retail stores and independent accounts.

Regional sales management. Where the seller has fewer, but scattered, major accounts, the best approach is often to assign each field sales manager to one or two accounts—an approach furniture and apparel businesses sometimes use. (However, this approach runs the risk that the sales manager will neglect managing in favor of selling.)

Small national account group. Even fewer major accounts can usually be handled by a small national structure of headquarters specialists. A large ink company, for example, uses several experienced, capable salespeople to call on the national publishers and printers that have many plants, while field salespeople call on individual plants.

There are many variations on this general approach. In some companies, especially industrial products manufacturers, market or product specialists or both fill the major account sales role. For instance, one manufacturer of complex specialized industrial materials has three selling organizations. These are (1) the regular field sales

force, which is organized geographically; (2) product
managers who are responsible for each general product
category, technically trained, and available to help the
field sales force with technical and applications problems for major sales; and (3) marketing managers who
are responsible for developing marketing programs for
major industry categories (like electronics and capital
equipment), who help handle major sales, and who participate in industry-oriented trade shows.

Separate division. Still others establish a separate
integrated division for the large accounts so that these
accounts can receive special attention from an integrated operation (such as manufacturing and marketing). While this is expensive and not easy to do, it
ensures that large sales will not disrupt normal plant
activities. This is a typical approach for companies that
manufacture private-label products for large retail
chains. Often these companies can reap special manufacturing savings by producing long runs and limited product lines in a separate, specially designed facility.

Top management. Finally, top executives make the
large sales in some companies. One large building cleaning and maintenance contractor, for example, has no real
field sales force. Instead, customer liaison people work
with existing customers. However, the real sales work
is done by top headquarters executives who deal with
owners and managers of large buildings.

   While this arrangement provides commitment and
organizational attention for the large accounts, it sometimes leads to neglect in the management of the business. The large accounts begin to demand more attention than the executives can spare.

COMPLETE INVOLVEMENT

On the other hand, nonrepetitive major sales are not handled by any established sales organization; a special sales force must be developed to handle them. The selling company has two options: It can develop a task force to handle the process internally, or it can contract with some form of sales agency, such as an investment banker, real estate or business broker, or private placement specialist.

If the sale is monumental (like the sale of the company), the task force must consist of people who have been removed from their other company responsibilities to as large an extent as possible. It should be put together carefully and include sales talent experienced in strategic selling and expert in finance (because of the complex nature and financial impact of such sales). In addition, people familiar with the prospective customers will be valuable to the team for their knowledge and possible personal contacts.

The nonrepetitive sales situation raises a unique training problem. Most of the learning must come through careful planning and review as the selling process is going on. However, salespeople can gain some training by working with people skilled in such sales situations (like investment bankers).

Nonrepetitive sales made by some form of facilitating sales organization, while expensive, decrease the drain on internal company resources. But even when outsiders take over much of the responsibility for the actual selling, company personnel need to be involved. Top managers don't always treat this kind of sale with the same expenditure of effort and resources as they treat other sales. They must choose the right agent—a difficult process that, to be done correctly, takes time. They must also supervise the selling process and ensure that the company's objectives are met with minimum expense. And finally, they are responsible for assisting in the actual sale, since their power and knowledge are often invaluable.

Elements of a Formal Presentation

Management Summary

TIES THE PRESENTATION to the individuals involved in the sale, reflects mutual agreement already reached with the top decision makers, and makes note of the customer's criteria for selection.

Scope

STATES THE OBJECTIVES and nature of the problems being solved or challenges being addressed.

Advantages

SPELLS OUT THE ADVANTAGES in such a way that the presenting company's products or services are made exclusive (so that they cannot be duplicated by competition).

Recommended Solutions

TAILORS THE SPECIFIC PRODUCTS, services, programs, or all three to the prospect's requirements, environment, and management objectives.

Financial Analysis and Cost Justification (reached through mutual agreement)

SHOWS THE ECONOMIC JUSTIFICATION to favor the seller company's method over the prospect's current means of performing the function and over possible proposals from competition.

Implementation Schedule

DESCRIBES THE seller's and the prospect's responsibilities, the people to be involved, and dates of completion for the main tasks.

Contract

SPELLS OUT THE TERMS and conditions of the sale, which have already been discussed with the prospect.

Note

1. For articles documenting this change, see "The New Supersalesman," *Business Week*, January 6, 1973; Alton F. Doody and William G. Nickels, "Structuring Organizations for Strategic Selling," *MSU Business Topics*, Autumn 1972; and Carl Rieser, "The Salesman Isn't Dead—He's Different," *Fortune*, November 1966.

Originally published in 1976
Reprint R0607L

Major Sales

Who Really Does the Buying?

THOMAS V. BONOMA

Executive Summary

WHEN IS A BUYER not really a buyer? How can the best product at the lowest price turn off buyers? Are there anonymous leaders who make the actual buying decisions? As these questions suggest, the reality of buying and selling is often not what it seems. What's more, salespeople often overlook the psychological and emotional factors that figure strongly in buying and selling. By failing to observe these less tangible aspects of selling, a vendor can lose sales without understanding why.

In this article, first published in 1982, Bonoma sets up a procedure for analyzing buying decisions and tells sellers how to apply the resulting framework to specific situations. Steps in the procedure include the following:

Identifying the actual decision makers. Though it may come as a surprise, power does not correlate perfectly with organizational rank. The author outlines five bases of power and offers six behavioral clues for identifying the real decision makers.

Determining how buyers view their self-interest. All buyers act selfishly, but they sometimes miscalculate. As a result, diagnosing motivation is one of the most difficult management tasks to do accurately. The author suggests several techniques to determine how buyers choose their own self-interest.

Gathering and applying psychological intelligence. There is no formula for placing sound psychological analyses magically in the sales staff's hands. However, the author offers three guidelines—make sure that sales calls are highly productive and informative, listen to the sales force, and reward rigorous fact gathering, analysis, and execution—to help managers increase sales effectiveness.

You don't understand: Willy was a salesman. . . . He don't put a bolt to a nut. He don't tell you the law or give you medicine. He's a man way out there in the blue, riding on a smile and a shoeshine. And when they start not smiling back—that's an earthquake.

—ARTHUR MILLER, *DEATH OF A SALESMAN*

MANY COMPANIES' SELLING EFFORTS are models of marketing efficiency. Account plans are carefully drawn, key accounts receive special management attention, and substantial resources are devoted to the sales process, from prospect identification to postsale service. Even such well-planned and well-executed selling strategies often fail, though, because management has an incomplete understanding of buying psychology—the human side of selling. Consider the following two examples:

A fast-growing maker and seller of sophisticated graphics computers had trouble selling to potentially major customers. Contrary to the industry practice of quoting high list prices and giving large discounts to users who bought in quantity, this company priced 10% to 15% lower than competitors and gave smaller quantity discounts. Even though its net price was often the lowest, the company met resistance from buyers. The reason, management later learned, was that purchasing agents measured themselves and were measured by their superiors less by the net price of the sophisticated computers they bought than by the amount deducted from the price during negotiations. The discount had a significance to buyers that sound pricing logic could not predict.

Several years ago, at AT&T's Long Lines division, an account manager was competing against a vendor with possibly better technology who threatened to lure away a key account. Among the customer's executives who might make the final decision about whether to switch from Bell were a telecommunications manager who had once been a Bell employee, a vice president of data processing who was known as a "big-name system buster" in his previous job because he had replaced all the IBM computers with other vendors' machines, and an aggressive telecommunications division manager who seemed to be unreachable by the AT&T team.

AT&T's young national account manager was nearly paralyzed by the threat. His team had never seriously considered the power, motivations, or perceptions of the various executives in the customer company, which had been buying from AT&T for many years. Without such analysis, effective and coordinated action on short notice—the usual time available for response to sales threats—was impossible.

Getting at the Human Factors

How can psychology be used to improve sales effectiveness? My contention is that seller awareness of and attention to the human factors in purchasing will produce higher percentages of completed sales and fewer unpleasant surprises in the selling process.

It would be inaccurate to call the human side of selling an emerging sales concern; only the most advanced companies recognize the psychology of buying as a major factor in improving account selection and selling results. Yet in most industries, the bulk of a company's business comes from a small minority of its customers. Retaining these key accounts is getting increasingly difficult as buyers constantly look not only for the best deal but also for the vendor that best understands them and their needs. It is this understanding and the targeted selling that results from it that can most benefit marketing managers.

BUYING A CORPORATE JET

The personal aspects and their complexities become apparent when one looks closely at an example of the buying process: the purchase of a business jet, which carries a price tag in excess of $3 million. The business-jet market splits obviously into two segments: those companies that already own or operate a corporate aircraft and those that do not.

In the owner market, the purchase process may be initiated by the chief executive officer, a board member (wishing to increase efficiency or security), the company's chief pilot, or through vendor efforts like advertising or a sales visit. The CEO will be central in deciding whether to buy the jet, but he or she will be heavily influenced by the company's pilot, financial officer, and perhaps by the board itself.

Each party in the buying process has subtle roles and needs. The salesperson who tries to impress, for example, both the CEO with depreciation schedules and the chief pilot with minimum runway statistics will almost certainly not sell a plane if he overlooks the psychological and emotional components of the buying decision. "For the chief executive," observes one salesperson, "you need all the numbers for support, but if you can't find the kid inside the CEO and excite him or her with the raw beauty of the new plane, you'll never sell the equipment. If you sell the excitement, you sell the jet."

The chief pilot, as an equipment expert, often has veto power over purchase decisions and may be able to stop the purchase of one or another brand of jet by simply expressing a negative opinion about, say, the plane's bad weather capabilities. In this sense, the pilot not only influences the decision but also serves as an information gatekeeper by advising management on the equipment to select. Though the corporate legal staff will formulate the purchase agreement and the purchasing department will acquire the jet, these parties may have little to say about whether or how the plane will be obtained, and which type. The users of the jet—middle and upper management of the buying company, important customers, and others—may have at least an indirect role in choosing the equipment.

The involvement of many people in the purchase decision creates a group dynamic that the selling company must factor into its sales planning. Who makes up the buying group? How will the parties interact? Who will dominate and who submit? What priorities do the individuals have?

It takes about three months for those companies that already own or operate aircraft to reach a decision. Because even the most successful vendor will sell no more than 90 jets a year, every serious prospect is a key account. The nonowners, not surprisingly, represent an even more complex market, since no precedent or aviation specialists exist.

The buying process for other pieces of equipment and for services will be more or less similar, depending on the company, product, and people involved. The purchase of computer equipment, for example, parallels the jet decision, except that sales prospects are likely to include data processing and production executives and the market is divided into small and large prospects rather than owners and non-owners. In other cases (such as upgrading the corporate communications network, making a fleet purchase, or launching a plant expansion), the buying process may be very different. Which common factors will reliably steer selling-company management toward those human considerations likely to improve selling effectiveness?

Different buying psychologies exist that make effective selling difficult. On the one hand, companies don't buy, people do. This knowledge drives the seller to analyze who the important buyers are and what they want. On the other hand, many individuals, some of whom may be unknown to the seller, are involved in most major purchases. Even if all the parties are identified, the outcome of their interaction may be unpredictable from knowledge of them as individuals. Effective selling requires usefully combining the individual and group dynamics of buying to predict what the buying "decision-making unit" will do. For this combination to be practical, the selling company must answer four key questions.

Question 1: Who's in the Buying Center?

The set of roles, or social tasks, buyers can assume is the same regardless of the product or participants in the purchase decision. This set of roles can be thought of as a fixed set of behavioral pigeonholes into which different managers from different functions can be placed to aid understanding. Together, the buying managers who take on these roles can be thought of as a "buying center."[1]

The exhibit "Members of the Buying Center and Their Roles" shows six buying roles encountered in every selling situation. I have illustrated these roles using the purchase or upgrading of a telecommunications system as an example. Let's consider each triangle, representing a buying role, in turn.

The *initiator* of the purchase process, whether for a jet, paper towels, or communication services, recognizes that some company problem can be solved or avoided by acquiring a product or service. A company's turbo-prop aircraft may provide neither the speed nor the range to get top management quickly to and from scattered operations. The prospective buyer of communications equipment may want to take advantage of technological improvements or to reduce costs through owning instead of leasing.

Members of the Buying Center and Their Roles

Initiator
Division general manager proposes to replace the company's telecommunications system

Decider
Vice president of administration selects, with influence from others, the vendor the company will deal with and the system it will buy

Influencers
Corporate telecommunications department and the vice president of data processing have important say about which system and vendor the company will deal with

Purchaser
Corporate purchasing department completes the purchase to specifications by negotiating or bidding

Gatekeeper
Corporate purchasing and corporate telecommunications departments analyze the company's needs and recommend likely matches with potential vendors

Users
All division employees who use the telecommunications equipment

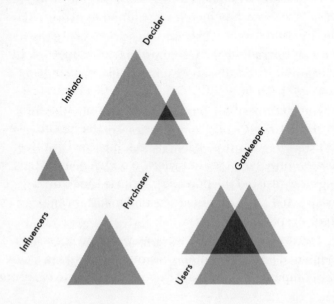

One or more *gatekeepers* are involved in the purchase process. These individuals, who may have the title of buyer or purchasing manager, usually act as problem or product experts. They are paid to keep up on the range of vendor offerings. In the jet example, the chief pilot will ordinarily fill this role. In the telecommunications example given in the exhibit, corporate purchasing, the corporate telecommunications staff, or, increasingly, data-processing experts may be consulted. By controlling (literally keeping the gate open or shut for) information and, sometimes, vendor access to corporate decision makers, the gatekeepers largely determine which vendors get the chance to sell. For some purchases the gatekeeping process is formalized through the use of an approved-vendors list, which constitutes a written statement of who can (and who, by absence, cannot) sell to the company.

Influencers are those who have a say in whether a purchase is made and about what is bought. The range of influencers becomes increasingly broad as major purchases are contemplated, because so many corporate resources are involved and so many people affected. In important decisions, board committees, stockholders of a public company, and even "lowly" mechanics can become influencers. One mining-machinery company encountered difficulty selling a new type of machine to its underground-mining customers. It turned out that mine maintenance personnel, who influenced the buying decision, resisted the purchase because they would have to learn to fix the new machine and maintain another stock of spare parts.

The *deciders* are those who say yes or no to the contemplated purchase. Often with major purchases, many of a company's senior managers act together to carry out the decider role. Ordinarily, however, one of these will become champion or advocate of the contemplated purchase and move it to completion. Without such a champion, many purchases would never be made. It is important to point out that deciders often do not sign off on purchases, nor do they make them. That is left to others. Though signers often represent themselves as deciders, such representation can be deceptive. It is possible for a vendor with a poor feel for the buying center never to become aware of the real movers in the buying company.

The purchase of executive computer workstations clearly illustrates both the importance of the champion and the behind-the-scenes role of the decider. A high-level executive who has become interested in using computers at his or her job after reading a magazine article or after tinkering with a home computer might decide to try out microcomputers or time-sharing terminals. The executive might then ask the company's data-processing group—which is likely to be quite resistant and averse to executive meddling—to evaluate available microcomputer equipment. When trial purchases are made, the high-level executive will quietly help steer the system through the proper channels leading to acceptance and further purchases. The vendor, dealing directly with the data-processing people, may never be aware that this decider exists.

The *purchaser* and the *user* are those concerned, respectively, with obtaining and consuming the product or service. The corporate purchasing department usually fills the purchaser role. Who fills the user role depends on the product or service.

Remember that I am discussing social roles, not individuals or groups of individuals. As such, the number of managers filling the buying roles varies from one to 35.

In very trivial situations, such as a manager's purchase of a pocket calculator on a business trip, one person will fill all six roles. The triangles in the exhibit would overlap: the manager initiates (perceives a need), "gatekeeps" (what brand did I forget at home?), influences himself or herself (this is more than I need, but it's only $39.95), decides, buys, and uses the equipment.

In more important buying situations, the number of managers assuming roles increases. In a study of 62 capital equipment and service acquisitions in 31 companies, Wesley J. Johnston and I quantified the buying center.[2] In the typical capital equipment purchase, an average of four departments (engineering and purchasing were always included), three levels of management hierarchy (for example, manager, regional manager, vice president), and seven different persons filled the six buying roles. For services, the corresponding numbers were four departments, two levels of management, and five managers. As might be expected, the more complex and involved the buying decision, the larger the decision unit and the more careful its decisions. For example, when packing supplies were ordered, little vendor searching or postsale evaluation was involved. When a new boiler was bought, careful vendor comparisons and postsale audits were undertaken.

Question 2: Who Are the Powerful Buyers?

As useful as the buying-center concept is, it is difficult to apply because managers do not wear tags that say "decision maker" or "unimportant person."[3] The powerful are often invisible, at least to vendor representatives.

Unfortunately, power does not correlate perfectly with organizational rank. As the case of the mine maintenance personnel illustrates, those with little formal power may be able to stop a purchase or hinder its completion. A purchasing manager who will not specify a disfavored vendor or the secretary who screens one vendor's salespeople because of a real or imagined slight also can dramatically change the purchasing outcome. Sales efforts cannot be directed through a simple reading of organizational charts; the selling company must identify the powerful buying-center members.

In the exhibit "Bases of Power," I outline five major power bases in the corporation. In addition, I have cate-

Bases of Power

Type of Power	Champion	or Veto
Reward Ability to provide monetary, social, political, or psychological rewards to others for compliance	■	
Coercive Ability to provide monetary or other punishments for noncompliance	■	
Attraction Ability to elicit compliance from others because they like you	■	■
Expert Ability to elicit compliance because of technical expertise, either actual or reputed		■
Status Compliance-gaining ability derived from a legitimate position of power in a company		■

Note: These five power bases were originally proposed over 20 years ago by psychologists J.R.P. French, Jr., and Bertram Raven. See "The Bases of Social Power" in D. Cartwright, ed., *Studies in Social Power* (University of Michigan Press, 1959).

gorized them according to whether their influence is positive (champion power) or negative (veto power).

Reward power refers to a manager's ability to encourage purchases by providing others with monetary, social, political, or psychological benefits. In one small company, for instance, the marketing vice president hoped to improve marketing decisions by equipping the sales force with small data-entry computers. Anticipating objections that the terminals were unnecessary, she felt forced to offer the sales vice president a computer of his own. The purchase was made.

Coercive power refers to a manager's ability to impose punishment on others. Of course, threatening punishment is not the same thing as having the power to impose it. Those managers who wave sticks most vigorously are sometimes the least able to deliver anything beyond a gentle breeze.

Attraction power refers to a person's ability to charm or otherwise persuade people to go along with his or her preferences. Next to the ability to reward and punish, attraction is the most potent power base in managerial life. Even CEOs find it difficult to rebut a key customer with whom they have flown for ten years who says, "Joe, as your friend, I'm telling you that buying this plane would be a mistake."

When a manager gets others to go along with his judgment because of real or perceived expertise in some area, *expert power* is being invoked. A telecommunications manager will find it difficult to argue with an acknowledged computer expert who contends that buying a particular telephone switching system is essential for the "office of the future"—or that not buying it now eventually will make effective communication impossible. With expert power, the skills need not be real, if by "real" we mean that the individual actually possesses what is attributed to him. It is enough that others believe that the expert has special skills or are willing to respect his opinion because of accomplishments in a totally unrelated field.

Status power comes from having a high position in the corporation. This notion of power is most akin to what is meant by the word "authority." It refers to the kind of influence a president has over a first-line supervisor and is more restricted than the other power bases. At first glance, status power might be thought of as similar to reward or coercive power. But it differs in significant ways. First, the major influence activity of those positions of corporate authority is persuasion, not punishment or reward. We jawbone rather than dangle carrots and taunt with sticks because others in the company also have significant power that they could invoke in retaliation.

Second, the high-status manager can exercise his or her status repeatedly only because subordinates allow it. In one heavy-manufacturing division, for example, the continual specification of favored suppliers by a plant manager (often at unfavorable prices) led to a "palace revolt" among other managers whose component cost evaluations were constantly made to look poor. Third, the power base of those in authority is very circumscribed since authority only tends to work in a downward direction on the organization chart and is restricted to specific work-related requests. Status power is one of the weaker power bases.

Buying centers and individual managers usually display one dominant power base in purchasing decisions. In one small company, an important factor is whether the manager arguing a position is a member of the founding family—a kind of status power and attraction power rolled into one. In a large high-technology defense contractor, almost all decisions are made on the basis of real or reputed expertise. This is true even when the issue under consideration has nothing to do with hardware or engineering science.

The key to improved selling effectiveness is in observation and investigation to understand prospects' corporate power culture. The sales team must also learn the type of power key managers in the buying company have or aspire to. Discounts or offers of price reductions may not be especially meaningful to a young turk in the buying company who is most concerned with status power; a visit by senior selling-company management may prove much more effective for flattering the ego and making the sale. Similarly, sales management may wish to make more technical selling appeals to engineers or other buying-company staff who base their power on expertise.

The last two columns of the exhibit show that the type of power invoked may allow the manager to support or to oppose a proposal, but not always both. I believe status and expert power are more often employed by their holders to veto decisions with which they do not agree. Because others are often "sold" on the contemplated purchase, vetoing it generally requires either the ability to perceive aspects not seen by the average manager because of special expertise or the broader view that high corporate status is said to provide. Reward and coercive power are more frequently used to push through purchases and the choice of favored vendors. Attraction power seems useful and is used by both champions and vetoers. The central point here is that for many buying-center members, power tends to be unidirectional.

SIX BEHAVIORAL CLUES

On the basis of the preceding analysis of power centers, I have distilled six clues for identifying the powerful:

1. Though power and formal authority often go together, the correlation between the two is not perfect. The selling company must take into account other clues about where the true buying power lies.

2. One way to identify buying-center power holders is to observe communications in the buying company. Of course, the powerful are not threatened by others, nor are they often promised rewards. Still, even the most powerful managers are likely to be influenced by others, especially by those whose power is based on attraction or expertise. Those with less power use persuasion and rational argument to try to influence the more powerful. Managers to whom others direct much attention but who receive few offers of rewards or threats of punishment usually possess substantial decision-making power.

3. Buying-center decision makers may be disliked by those with less power. Thus, when others express concern about one buying-center member's opinions along with their feelings of dislike or ambivalence, sellers have strong clues as to who the powerful buyer is.

4. High-power buyers tend to be one-way information centers, serving as focal points for information from others. The vice president who doesn't come to meetings but who receives copies of all correspondence about a buying matter is probably a central influencer or decider.

5. The most powerful buying-center members are probably not the most easily identified or the most talkative members of their groups. Indeed, the really powerful buying group members often send others to critical negotiations because they are confident that little of substance will be made final without their approval.

6. No correlation exists between the functional area of a manager and his or her power within a company. It is not possible to approach the data-processing department blindly to find decision makers for a new computer system, as many sellers of mainframes have learned. Nor can one simply look to the CEO to find a decision maker for a corporate plane. There is no substitute for working hard to understand the dynamics of the buying company.

Question 3: What Do They Want?

Diagnosing motivation accurately is one of the easiest management tasks to do poorly and one of the most difficult to do well. Most managers have lots of experience at diagnosing another's wants, but though the admission comes hard, most are just not very accurate when trying to figure out what another person wants and will do. A basic rule of motivation is as follows: All buyers (indeed, all people) act selfishly or try to be selfish but sometimes miscalculate and don't serve their own interests. Thus, buyers attempt to maximize their gains and minimize their losses from purchase situations. How do buyers choose their own self-interest? The following are insights into that decision-making process from research.

First, buyers act as if a complex product or service were decomposable into various benefits. Examples of benefits might include product features, price, reliability, and so on.

Second, buyers segment the potential benefits into various categories. The most common of these are financial, product-service, social-political, and personal. For some buyers, the financial benefits are paramount, while for others, the social-political ones—how others in the company will view the purchase—rank highest. Of course, the dimensions may be related, as when getting the lowest-cost product (financial) results in good performance evaluations and a promotion (social-political).

Finally, buyers ordinarily are not certain that purchasing the product will actually bring the desired benefit. For example, a control computer sold on its reliability and industrial-strength construction may or may not fulfill its promise. Because benefits have value only if they actually are delivered, the buyer must be confident that the selling company will keep its promises. Well-known vendors, like IBM or Xerox, may have some advantage over lesser-known companies in this respect.

As marketers know, not all promised benefits will be equally desired by all customers. All buyers have top-priority benefit classes, or "hot buttons." For example, a telecommunications manager weighing a choice between Bell and non-Bell equipment will find some benefits, like ownership, available only from non-Bell vendors. Other desired benefits, such as reputation for service and reliability, may be available to a much greater degree from Bell. The buyer who has financial priorities as a hot button may decide to risk possible service-reliability problems for the cost-reduction benefits available through ownership. Another manager—one primarily concerned with reducing the social-political risks that result from service problems—may reach a different decision. The exhibit "Dominant Motives for Buying a Telecommunications System" schematically shows the four classes into which buyers divide benefits. The telecommunications example illustrates each class.

Outlining the buyer's motivation suggests several possible selling approaches. The vendor can try to focus the buyer's attention on benefits not a part of his or her thinking. A magazine sales representative, for instance, devised a questionnaire to help convince an uncertain client to buy advertising space. The questionnaire sought information about the preferred benefits—in terms of reach, audience composition, and cost per thousand readers. When the prospective buyer "played this silly game" and filled out the questionnaire, he convinced

---

Dominant Motives for Buying a Telecommunications System

The benefits in the shaded column are more highly valued than the others and represent the company's "hot button."

Benefit Class

Financial	Product or Service	Social or Political	Personal
Absolute cost savings	Pre- and post-sales service	Will purchase enhance the buyer's standing with the buying team or top management?	Will purchase increase others' liking or respect for the buyer?
Cheaper than competitive offerings	Specific features		
Will provide operating-cost reductions	Space occupied by unit		How does purchase fit with buyer's self-concept?
Economics of leasing versus buying	Availability		

himself of the superior worth of the vendor's magazine on the very grounds he was seeking to devalue it.

Conversely, sellers can de-emphasize the buyer's desire for benefits on which the vendor's offering stacks up poorly. For example, if a competing vendor's jet offers better fuel economy, the selling company might attempt to refocus the buyer's attention toward greater speed or lower maintenance costs.

The vendor can also try to increase the buyer's confidence that promised benefits will be realized. One software company selling legal administrative systems, for example, provides a consulting service that remote users can phone if they are having problems, backup copies of its main programs in case users destroy the original, a complete set of input forms to encourage full data entry, and regular conferences to keep users current on system revisions. These services are designed to bolster the confidence of extremely conservative administrators and lawyers who are shopping for a system.

Finally, vendors often try to change what the buyer wants or which class of benefits he or she responds to most strongly. My view of motivation suggests that such an approach is almost always unsuccessful. Selling strategy needs to work with the buyer's motivations, not around them.

Question 4: How Do They Perceive Us?

How buyers perceive the selling company, its products, and its personnel is very important to efficient selling. Powerful buyers invariably have a wide range of perceptions about a vending company. One buyer will have a friend at another company who has used a similar product and claimed that "it very nearly ruined us." Another may have talked to someone with a similar product who claims that the vending company "even sent a guy out on a plane to Hawaii to fix the unit there quickly. These people really care."

One drug company representative relates the story of how the company was excluded from all the major metropolitan hospitals in one city because a single influential physician believed that one of the company's new offerings was implicated in a patient's death. This doctor not only generalized his impressions to include all the company's products but encouraged his friends to boycott the company.

A simple scheme for keeping tabs on how buyers perceive sellers is to ask sales officials to estimate how the important buyers judge the vending company and its actions. This judgment can be recorded on a continuum ranging from negative to positive. If a more detailed judgment is desired, the selling company can place its products and its people on two axes perpendicular to each other, like this:

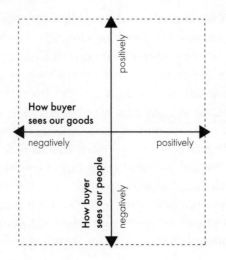

The scarcity of marketing dollars and the effectiveness of champions in the buying process argue strongly for focusing resources where they are likely to do the most good. Marketing efforts should aim at those in the buying company who like the selling company, since they are partially presold. While there is no denying the adage, "It's important to sell everybody," those who diffuse their efforts this way often sell no one.

Gathering Psychological Intelligence

While I would like to claim that some new technique will put sound psychological analyses magically in your sales staff's hands, no such formula exists. But I have used the human-side approach in several companies to increase sales effectiveness, and there are only three guidelines needed to make it work well.

MAKE PRODUCTIVE SALES CALLS A NORM, NOT AN ODDITY

Because of concern about the rapidly rising cost of a sales call, managers are seeking alternative approaches to selling. Sales personnel often do not have a good idea of why they are going on most calls, what they hope to find out, and which questions will give them the needed answers. Sales-call planning is not only a matter of minimizing miles traveled or courtesy calls on unimportant prospects but of determining what intelligence is needed about key buyers and what questions or requests are likely to produce that information.

I recently traveled with a major account representative of a duplication equipment company, accompanying him on the five calls he made during the day. None of the visits yielded even 10% of the potential psychological or other information that the representative could use on future calls, despite the fact that prospects made such information available repeatedly.

At one company, for example, we learned from a talkative administrator that the CEO was a semirecluse who insisted on approving equipment requests himself; that one of the divisional managers had (without the agreement of the executive who was our host) brought in a competitor's equipment to test; and that a new duplicator the vendor had sold to the company was more out of service than in. The salesperson pursued none of this freely offered information, nor did he think any of it important enough to write down or pass on to the sales manager. The call was wasted because the salesperson didn't know what he was looking for or how to use what was offered him.

The exhibit "Matrix for Gathering Psychological Information" shows a matrix that can be used to capture on a single sheet of paper essential psychological data about a customer. I gave some clues for filling

---

Matrix for Gathering Psychological Information

Who's in the buying center, and what is the base of their power?	
Who are the powerful buyers, and what are their priorities?	
What specific benefits does each important buyer want?	
How do the important buyers see us?	
Selling strategy	

in the matrix earlier in the article, but how sales representatives go about gathering the information depends on the industry, the product, and especially the customer. In all cases, however, key selling assessments involve (1) isolating the powerful buying-center members, (2) identifying what they want in terms of both their hot buttons and specific needs, and (3) assessing their perceptions of the situation. Additionally, gathering psychological information is more often a matter of listening carefully than of asking clever questions during the sales interview.

LISTEN TO THE SALES FORCE

Nothing discourages intelligence gathering as much as the sales force's conviction that management doesn't really want to hear what salespeople know about an account. Many companies require the sales force to file voluminous call reports and furnish other data—which vanish, never to be seen or even referred to again unless a sales representative is to be punished for one reason or another.

To counter this potentially fatal impediment, I recommend a sales audit. Evaluate all sales force control forms and call reports and discard any that have not been used by management for planning or control purposes in the last year. This approach has a marvelously uplifting effect all around; it frees the sales force from filling in forms it knows nobody uses, sales management from gathering forms it doesn't know what to do with, and data processing from processing reports no one ever requests. Instead, use a simple, clear, and accurate sales control form of the sort suggested in the matrix exhibit—preferably on a single sheet of paper for a particular sales period. These recommendations may sound drastic, but where management credibility in gathering and using sales force intelligence is absent, drastic measures may be appropriate.

EMPHASIZE HOMEWORK AND DETAILS

Having techniques for acquiring sales intelligence and attending to reports is not enough. Sales management must stress that yours is a company that rewards careful fact gathering, tight analysis, and impeccable execution. This message is most meaningful when it comes from the top.

Cautionary Notes

The group that influences a purchase doesn't call itself a buying center. Nor do decision makers and influencers think of themselves in those terms. Managers must be careful not to mistake the analysis and ordering process for the buyers' actions themselves. In addition, gathering data such as I have recommended is a sensitive issue. For whatever reasons, it is considered less acceptable to make psychological estimates of buyers than economic ones. Computing the numbers without understanding the psychology, however, leads to lost sales. Finally, the notion implicit throughout this article has been that sellers must understand buying, just as buyers must understand selling. When that happens, psychology and marketing begin to come together usefully. Closed sales follow almost as an afterthought.

Notes

1. The concept of the buying center was proposed in its present form by Frederick E. Webster, Jr., and Yoram Wind in *Organizational Buying Behavior* (Prentice-Hall, 1972).

2. Wesley J. Johnston and Thomas V. Bonoma, "Purchase Process for Capital Equipment and Services," *Industrial Marketing Management*, vol. 10, 1981.

3. In the interest of saving space, I will not substantiate each reference to psychological research. Documentation for my assertions can be found in Thomas V. Bonoma and Gerald Zaltman, *Management Psychology* (Kent Publishing, 1981). See Chapter 8 for the power literature and Chapter 3 for material on motivation.

Originally published in 1982
Reprint R0607P

Humanize Your Selling Strategy

HARVEY B. MACKAY

Executive Summary

IS THERE AN INDUSTRY that's more of a commodity business than envelopes? It's hard to differentiate yourself when you're selling envelopes, but Mackay Envelope Corporation of Minneapolis has gained steadily in sales and market share by stressing salesmanship—inspired, energized, superior salesmanship.

Through building personal relationships and through research, Mackay develops elaborate files on customers and potential customers—not only business data but also information on each contact's education, family, particular interests, and life-style. The goal is to focus on the *individual* across the table. The relationship resembles a marriage in the attention the salesperson pays to little things, like obtaining a Rose Bowl program for the Michigan football fan whose team was playing there on New Year's Day.

149

Such attention to detail requires well-trained, alert salespeople. Harvey Mackay himself spends evenings with candidates and their spouses and tests them with long telephone conversations. Once hired, they routinely take Dale Carnegie and Toastmasters courses. These teach the salespeople to listen and speak well. The company rewards top performers for collaborative work as well as for landing big contracts.

You can't be Number One with every customer or potential customer. But you can win the confidence of a lot of them, so that if something happens to the number one supplier, as Number Two, you're next in line. Good leadership from the top and recognition of stellar sales performance yield a focused selling strategy—the best way to pump volume and boost market share.

YOU ARE SITTING in a conference room with your marketing manager and sales staff, engaged in reviewing the account of a key customer. To begin her analysis, the account executive opens up the file folder and reads aloud:

"Staunch Republican"

"Midwestern value system"

"Enthusiastic booster of the Boy Scouts"

"Avid stamp collector"

"Procrastinates on major buying decisions . . . needs strong follow-through"

Of course, the report also includes data on the market position, new product lines, and plans for factory construction of the customer's company. But a sizable portion of the discussion focuses on the customer's personal chemistry and characteristics . . . and how well the salesperson understands these traits and creatively markets to them. Sound like a peculiar use of management time? For many marketers such a discussion would border on the unorthodox, but companies that ignore such vital and revealing information are at a distinct disadvantage in the marketplace.

Many companies are becoming ever more adept at using segmented marketing strategies. In mere seconds, video and print messages can establish instant rapport with a targeted customer. But in the meantime, businesses have lost sight of the need to humanize their selling strategies. Computerized purchase orders, rampant cost analysis, and sophisticated financial modeling have overwhelmed the salesperson-corporate customer relationship.

Envelopes are not a glamorous business. In fact, they are about as drab a commodity as you can imagine—in what is nearly the textbook definition of a mature industry. That means you have to be especially good at differentiating your company if you expect to gain market share. In the envelope industry, Mackay's products are constantly being assaulted by newer, sexier, more convenient ways to communicate, like telephones and computers and electronic mail. A company's margins can be paper thin.

Despite these drawbacks, in the past five years Mackay Envelope has seen its sales volume rise an average 18% a year to $35 million, and its market share rise to 2% nationally (pretty good in this fragmented industry; there are 235 envelope companies in the country). Mackay has also become one of the most profitable companies in the industry. We credit our success to one factor more than any other: salesmanship—inspired, energized, superior salesmanship.

For years it was fashionable for U.S. executives with any decent pedigree to sneer at sales, the land of Willy Loman. But today we are beginning to see a mighty re-direction of the resources of the American corporation. Head counts in administration, production, and R&D are dwindling, but sales forces are on the rise. When IBM announced it would trim its staff by 12,000 by the end of 1987, it simultaneously reassigned 3,000 people to its sales force. The transformation of Campbell Soup from a gray lady to a leading business innovator is largely attributed to a new marketing strategy that has focused on targeting and selling to sharply defined customer niches. Former Porsche CEO Peter Schutz, in an inter-view in this publication two years ago, stressed how much time he spent in the Porsche delivery room talking with customers and learning about their motivations and idiosyncracies.[1]

At Mackay Envelope we use every means we can think of to exalt selling and salespeople. The parking place just outside the door of the main office is not reserved for the CEO. Above it is this sign:

Reserved for
[we fill in the name]
Salesperson of the Month.

This is our way of declaring to our 350 employees, our visitors, and the world at large that sales are at the very heart of our business.

During speaking engagements at management semi-nars from Athens to New Delhi, I have talked with opera-tors of myriad other businesses, from truffles and textiles to trucks and high technology. The problems and chal-lenges I have heard described are extraordinarily similar, and most of them turn on a failure to manage selling fundamentals. Use of a few simple tactics and disciplines can alleviate many problems.

Know Your Customer . . . in Spades

In a one-hour lunch you can learn everything from a golf handicap to views on the federal deficit, from size of home to favorite vacation spot. "So what?" I've heard people say. "It's hard enough to remember my sales and inventory turnover from last month. Why should I clutter my brain and my files with this new version of Trivial Pursuit?" Because it establishes you as an effective listener, that's why. Effective listeners remember order dates and quality specifications. They are easier to talk with when there's a problem with a shipment. In short, effective listeners sell more customers . . . and keep them longer.

For 27 years at Mackay, we have used a device to get people to record and review this kind of data. It's a questionnaire form. People inside our company have taken to calling it the "Mackay 66" (because it has 66 questions). We complete at least one on every customer. It lists all the vital statistics we gather, such as our contact's educational background, career history, family, special interests, and life-style. It's continually updated and it's studied to death in our company. Our overriding goal is to know more about our customers than they know about themselves.

I've had people ask me, "Don't you feel like the FBI or the KGB, running dossiers on your customers?" I don't. The questionnaire is merely a system for organizing what the best executives and salespeople have done for a long time: demonstrate exceptional understanding of their customers as people.

The point here is that people don't truly care how much you know until they know how much you care. One purpose of the Mackay 66 is to empower the perceptive and empathetic salesperson with information that, channeled properly, produces a response that says "I care."

For example, question number 48 asks about the customer's vacation habits. These say a lot about people. Is he the outdoors type who loves to white-water raft on the Colorado or camp out at Yosemite? Does she like to tour Europe and Japan by bus? Is she a tennis enthusiast who plans her vacations around major professional tournaments?

How would that lover of the outdoors react to a book of photographs of Yosemite by Ansel Adams? What would the sightseeing type say on receiving an array of hard-to-get brochures of unusual and exotic tours? Imagine the reaction of that tennis buff as she reads previews of Wimbledon and the U.S. Open we sent her a few weeks before those events.

Each of these instances happened. The donor wasn't a husband, wife, friend, or neighbor but a Mackay account executive. Were these gestures perceived as insincere? They could have been, but they weren't. They represented actions taken after seller and buyer had achieved a certain level of communication and rapport. The best salespeople are "other conscious." They're sensitive people who are genuinely interested in others. They don't do things to people; they do things *for* people, after they've learned something about those people.

Who were the sources of information regarding the vacation habits? They could have been secretaries, receptionists, or other suppliers. They often are. In these situations, however, they were the prospective customers themselves. The information about vacations was cross-

referenced to question number 51, "conversational interests." In each instance, this information was culled from
the customer over breakfast or lunch (naturally, after the
name of the customer's favorite restaurant was elicited
from the secretary).

When the little gift came, it arrived on the prospective
customer's birthday (the date is asked in question number 5), long after that introductory lunch or breakfast.
Was the customer aware that the giver had an ulterior
motive? Yes, in part. But what also came across was the
salesperson's thoughtfulness and sincere desire to establish a solid, long-term relationship. The personal touch is
so rare a commodity today, it becomes a standout. Does
it always translate into new business? Not always, but
often; and not always immediately, but eventually.

I learned the impact of using one's intelligence on
customers when, as a young constituent, I walked into
Senator Hubert Humphrey's Washington office for the
first time and he amazed me by showing he knew about
my goals and avocations. Although we had only a brief
conversation, his genuine likability and superior information turned me into a friend, a supporter, and a loyal
contributor. The intent is not to get something on some-
body. The goal is to pay attention to the *person* across
the table. Salespeople sell to people, not computer terminals. I have found that salespeople who can't understand
and empathize with the goals of the people they sell to
are incapable of understanding and empathizing with
the goals of the broader organization they later have to
serve in filling the order.

At any big social function you see effective top executives creating mental profiles on the people they meet.
Leaders learn to pay attention to what's important in
other people's lives. That means keeping your antennae

up and noticing the details. It's not manipulation but disarmament. All of us are naturally hostile to persuasion and salesmanship. Well, everyone whose livelihood relies on making a sale had better learn to neutralize that hostility, so he or she can get on with the business of honestly selling the product. Our format simplifies the method and puts it into the hands of the little guy. With practice and a modicum of discipline, anyone can master the skill of harvesting customer awareness.

Once each year, our marketing people and our top operating people sit down and review the material on our key customers, with special emphasis on the last page—the page that deals with the customer's view of the goals and issues facing that company's management, as stated to our salespeople. This analysis of common customer issues is the launching pad for our planning.

When a salesperson quits or retires, it is very difficult to sustain valuable personal relationships in business-to-business selling. But these continually updated files have allowed us to put a new client contact into position far faster than most businesses can. The greatest danger when you lose a veteran salesperson is, of course, that the client will be spirited away too. The documentation that the salesperson has built up (often over years) gives us a big edge in establishing a lasting relationship between the new Mackay account representative and the customer.

Ask the salespeople in any company, "Are you dealing with the same purchasing agent at Jones & Smith today as you were five years ago?" The answer is quite probably no. In international businesses especially, purchasing people are transferred often. Therefore, make a point of getting to know the whole department—especially the up-and-comers—and learn the company's practices on moving people. In short, dig your well before you're thirsty.

As a manager, I judge the intensity and the discipline of our 20-plus salespeople by looking at how up-to-date their customer profiles are. Scanning the profile is stage one of any account review. Sometimes a superficially completed profile or one filled with awkward hedges is a godsend of an early warning. It can signal a salesperson mismatch with an account. And *that* means a switch in account assignments before the customer decides to take a hike.

As important as the questionnaire is, it's vital not to confuse the form with the mind-set and discipline it represents. The form is just a tool to readjust people's vision. You and I have both sat across the table from too many salespeople whose eyes became glazed over with indifference, whose sighs of boredom betrayed their thought, which was: "Just sign the order, you're wasting my time"—as if you, the customer, were obligated to help boost the caller's profits. The method built around the questionnaire arms the seller with superior information and intelligence and inspires a positive attitude toward making the sale.

A salesperson never has to make a cold call. Ever. Granted you aren't likely to learn much about family background and career history until you actually have your first meeting, but there is no reason you can't become an instant expert on a prospect company in advance. If it's a public company, your broker can round up an annual report and may be able to offer valuable insights too. I own at least one share of stock in every publicly traded company that is a customer. The public library is a powerful information arsenal, with countless business periodicals and readers' guides for tracking articles down. D&B reports are readily available and highly informative, but I think their existence must be "one of the best kept secrets" in U.S. business. The prospect's own customers, its other suppliers, and even former employees all can be fertile sources.

Ask your friendly banker. "Isn't that breaching a confidence?" you ask. Not if your banker doesn't happen to be your customer's banker too. Then there's the chamber of commerce buyer's guide. (Every chamber has one.) You can even subscribe to a clipping service to monitor the local and trade press. The list of easily available background sources is nearly endless.

This research requires the same skills that went into writing a good term paper. But so few people think of applying these disciplines in a sales situation. So many people close the door on their education and training and don't even think of using in real life what they spent dozens of years learning. The best business recruits recognize that their real education doesn't begin until they enter the workplace—because then education becomes application. I constantly remind my people that knowledge doesn't become power until it's used. That's why we use the "Mackay 66." That's why we write it all down.

In 33 years of selling, I have never called on a buyer I haven't sold. In that I'm not exceptional. The diligence and perseverance of our company's selling strategy are, however, unusual. Hardly anyone ever makes a sale on the first call. That's just as true for us as anyone else. Not every lead qualifies as a legitimate prospect. But when we decide that we want a company's envelope business, we've ultimately made the sale in virtually every case.

Years ago, as the business was building, I (as CEO) made the first call on most major prospects, and that call was invariably brief. I asked for 300 seconds of my counterpart's time, and usually the meeting lasted no more than 180 seconds. "We very much want to be your supplier," I'd say. "It means a lot to us. Here's what we can do. . . ." My comments were confined to differentiators like price, quality, service, or delivery time—whatever distinguished us from the competing supplier.

Courtship and Marriage

Many CEOs were terrific salespeople at early stages of their careers. But too often, after being installed in carpeted corner offices at headquarters, they have allowed a distance to grow between themselves and the sales arena. Then the CEO's only selling involvement takes place behind closed doors, pitching the board on a strategic plan or the executive committee on a management succession scenario.

That's a big mistake. Salespeople need to see the top people out there, mixing it up, setting the example. That's a prime reason why some of America's most visible chief executives, the Frank Perdues and Victor Kiams and Lee Iacoccas, are so effective when they get out in public to pitch their products on national television. They're not just selling products. They're also motivating their people to sell the products. Selling chickens may not be the most pleasant job in the world, but if the boss thinks it's important enough to do himself, then maybe it's important for the chicken salesperson too.

Most initial contacts are lengthy presentations with glowing claims concocted for audiences that are often too large and too highly placed. They abuse the customer's time. You don't need a Wagnerian epic to communicate a persuasive message. After all, the Gettysburg Address has only 270 words and the Lord's Prayer, a mere 54.

The follow-up happens on the technical level. What the CEO as salesperson should be selling is not product. It is a strategic idea . . . and it is trust.

The relationship is just like a marriage: small shows of sensitivity and awareness keep the spice in it. We have one customer whose version of heaven is salmon fishing in Scotland. You can bet that at least once a year an article on salmon angling from a fine British sporting magazine shows up on his desk, together with a handwritten note. A prospective customer, whom we have pursued for a year and a half, makes a pilgrimage to New York twice a year to feast on operas and concerts. Each September this client receives, in a Mackay envelope, the Carnegie Hall and Lincoln Center season programs. The personal touch is noticeably changing his attitude toward us.

We have a customer who is a University of Michigan alumnus and a passionate Wolverine football fan. In 1986, Michigan won the Big Ten football title. My secretary found out where Rose Bowl programs were being printed, ordered a copy, and had it sent to him. He was unable to attend the game on New Year's Day, but I'm sure he sat in front of his living room TV with that program clutched in his hands.

It takes time. Strategic, humanized selling always does. It is also based on very self-evident precepts . . . astonishingly simple. As the Prussian strategist Karl von Clausewitz wrote in *On War:* "Everything in strategy is very simple, but that does not mean everything is very easy."

Care and Feeding of Salespeople

The stereotype of the huckster who cajoles his mark into resigned submission—that portrait is one for the business history books. Today's seller must understand modern communication styles and concepts. That begins with knowing when to close one's mouth and open one's ears, but it entails a whole lot more.

Before we hire a salesperson, I always socialize with the candidate and the spouse. Too many important deals are secured in a social setting, like the ballpark or the ballet, for ease in handling contacts to be ignored. It's also important to see a candidate in his or her home setting. Is what you find at all like what you were told it would be? That is, is this person a straight shooter or prone to exaggeration? You don't want to learn later that a decade-long customer has been victimized by overpromises. I make a point of having a long telephone conversation with the candidate and sprinkling it with awkward pauses just to see how he or she handles them. Given the amount of business transacted by phone these days, you had better find out if you're signing up Ted Koppel or Archie Bunker.

We send our salespeople through Dale Carnegie or Toastmasters training because these courses emphasize how important listening is to effective speaking. Any outstanding public speaker will tell you that a speech is nothing more or less than the sale of an idea. The best speakers anchor their skills by monitoring audience feedback, from body language to the cough count.

Our constant exposure to electronic media has changed the way we expect to be persuaded. Persuaders must get to the point faster, speak in a vivid and engaging way, and blend their pitches so cleverly with customized information that it never sounds like mere patter.

An entire industry, insurance, has been built on the Law of Large Numbers. There are 264 million living Americans. The insurance people can predict within one-fourth of 1% how many of us will die within the next 12 months. They can tell us where, and how, in what age bracket, and of what sex, race, and profession. The only thing they can't predict is who. The sales force must apply this same principle to its prospect lists. If the lists are long enough, there will be salespeople for Number One suppliers who retire or die, or lose their territories for a hundred other reasons.

What you can't predict is which of your competitors will succumb to the Law of Large Numbers. But fortunately, as in the insurance business, which one doesn't matter. All that matters is that your salespeople have the perseverance and patience to position your company as Number Two to enough prospects. If they're standing second in line in enough lines, sooner or later they will move up to Number One.

In our company, we recognize that the kind of dogged persistence and patience it takes to convert a Number Two position to a Number One position is very tough for the typical salesperson to master. By nature, salespeople tend to be more like racehorses than plowhorses. The instant gratification syndrome that gets a salesperson to the finish line first is an ingrained part of the salesperson's makeup. That's why we insist on the customer profiles, the follow-ups, the disciplined account review, and, most of all, the emphasis on human sensitivity. Doubtless, it is not the fanciest marketing management system, but it is uncommonly effective for managing salespeople.

Let me illustrate by passing on a conversation I had with a young salesperson named Phil (I'll call him). It was like a lot of talks I've had with my salespeople over the years. Phil came into my office looking agitated.

Phil. Mr. Mackay, I need your help. I've been wrestling for over a year now to get the account at International Transom, and it's just no use. I think I'd better give up.

Mackay (*motions him toward a chair*). They buy from Enveloping Envelope, don't they?

Phil (*sits*). Yes, for seven years, and they don't have the slightest interest in changing suppliers. I think it's time for me to write off this particular prospect and spend my time on business with greater promise.

Mackay. International Transom is a very attractive account, Phil. I wonder if you're not chasing the wrong goal. Accept for now that they're happy with EE. Your objective isn't to become their supplier overnight; it's to become the undisputed holder of second place. (*Phil looks skeptical, so Mackay proceeds to explain the Law of Large Numbers.*)

Phil (*gloomily*). Based on what I've seen in calling on Bystrom, the purchasing agent at International Transom, it's going to be a long wait.

Mackay. I see you've got the customer profile there. Let me take a look. (*Phil hands him the folder. Mackay reads it.*) Aha. Just as I thought. This questionnaire reads like a dry and pretty spotty profile on someone you find intimidating, if not a little hostile. There's no vitality, no real grasp of the customer or his motivation. It's lifeless.

Phil (*agitated again*). But this guy is a clam, not at all outgoing.

Mackay (*sternly*). Did you read his desk? Were there any mementos there that told you something about him? How about plaques on the wall? What's his alma mater?

If he's businesslike with you, what are his aspirations? How does he identify with company goals? You don't have in here a recent article or current analyst's report on this company. (*Arises from his desk and gesticulates as he paces to and fro.*) How well have you shown him that you know and admire his company? That you know how it fits in its industry? Do you know the strengths and weaknesses of Enveloping Envelope in terms of International Transom? Have you emphasized to Bystrom those strengths that Mackay has almost exclusively, like centralized imprinting?

Phil. Well, I. . . .

Mackay. Have you, in short, made Bystrom feel absolutely terrible about not buying from you right now? Terrible because you are so knowledgeable, aware, interested in him as a person, and representing a company that is clearly differentiated from EE in important and positive ways?

Phil (*looking more excited now than upset*). I see what you mean, Mr. Mackay. You're asking me to aspire to the Number Two position, if we can't be first. Instead of telling me to win, you're telling me to prepare to win.

Mackay (*patting Phil on the back as they move toward the office door*). Exactly, Phil. (*He beams at Phil.*) You've got the right idea.

IT WASN'T LONG before Phil's folder on his prospect sharpened and fattened considerably. In this he had a lot of help, by the way, from others at Mackay Envelope who knew International Transom, Bystrom, and Enveloping Envelope. We have a reward system that recognizes outstanding individual performers and reinforces collaborative behavior. We don't focus on just the top salesperson. Each month we also reward the best networking that leads to a sale. We recognize a salesperson whose persistence has paid off with substantial new business. We spotlight a salesperson whose customer or competitive insight produced a significant change in the way we do business.

Your Selling Strategy

My definition of a great salesperson is not someone who can get the order. Anyone can get the order if he or she is willing to make enough promises about price or delivery time or service. A great salesperson is someone who can get the order—and the reorder— from a prospect who is already doing business with someone else. No salespeople can aspire to that kind of selling unless they are prepared to think strategically and humanistically about their customers. The beauty of it is, though, that with patience and some simple tools, you don't have to be a strategic genius or a management psychologist to excel.

If, however, you are a CEO or a manager who determines the climate and attitudes in your company, then I counsel you strongly to ensure that selling and salespeople in your organization get proper leadership and the recognition they deserve. No matter how many strides you make in product quality or asset management or new design features, there is no tool more likely to harm or help your market share than your selling strategy. This is a lesson companies can learn on their own initiative . . . or, I have no doubt, they will learn at the hands of their competitors.

Note

1. David E. Gumpert, "Porsche on Nichemanship," HBR
   March–April 1986, p. 98.

Originally published in March–April 1988
Reprint 88208

Manage the Customer, Not Just the Sales Force

Executive Summary

THE SUBJECT OF SALES MANAGEMENT has many
parts, each of them very important. One of the tasks of
the sales manager is to see these parts in perspective
and to understand their relationships. If, as so often happens, one activity or group of activities is magnified out
of proportion, the overall goals of management are
bound to suffer. This article discusses the four key areas
of sales management: defining the role of personal selling, deploying the sales force, managing the accounts,
and understanding the selling costs.

Recently i investigated the sales management problems of an apparel company that I will refer to by the fictitious name of Fitwell. At that time, the Fitwell Company had 50 salespeople and sales of $40 million in the medium to medium-high priced dress lines. The salespeople were paid on a variable commission rate, receiving 7% on dresses with a high gross margin for Fitwell and down to 5% on dresses with the lowest gross margin. The salespeople called on retail stores, paid their own out-of-pocket expenses, and averaged about $46,000 each in gross compensation per year.

A few years ago Fitwell introduced a higher priced dress line to keep pace with the market and to improve its margins. The line did not sell well despite its apparently fashion-right design, relatively heavy advertising, and extra high commissions (9%). The top executives who had developed the concept of the line were personally chagrined by the results.

The immediate reaction of Fitwell's sales managers was to push harder. The annual sales meeting included speeches by the chairman of the board, the president, the marketing vice president, and the national sales manager on the importance of the new line to the company and to the salespeople. The sales managers urged their regional managers to motivate their salespeople to "push the line." Contests were developed (e.g., a trip to Europe for the salesperson with the largest percentage of sales in the higher priced line and an automobile for the person with the largest total dollar volume). The more the sales managers "motivated," the more they frustrated themselves. Sales did not improve, and increasingly "powerful" speeches were met with frequent yawns.

The Fitwell Company's determination to motivate its salespeople to "push the line" is typical of the misplaced emphasis that occurs all through the business world. Too often top management thinks that motivation is the key to getting its people to follow a particular policy. However, management would be better off reevaluating its policy rather than focusing on motivating its employees, since often the problem is that top management has failed to develop an appropriate policy to begin with.

Let me hasten to say that the emphasis on managing the sales force is understandable. Since most sales managers—even national sales managers and sales vice presidents—were once active salespeople themselves, they naturally regard the sales force from the point of view of a salesperson. They ask, "How can we get more cooperation and more selling from the sales force?" But they do not ask, "How can we generate greater sales and profits?"

Sales managers sometimes forget that sales and profits are generated by the customer and that their objective is the management of the customer through the sales program, which is in turn implemented by the sales force. Their misplaced emphasis is serious because when they face problems like decreasing sales or market share, they change the means of managing the sales force but not its purpose.

Typically, sales managers change the compensation scheme, the most visible and talked about part of sales force management and the one which can be altered most rapidly. After monkeying around with compensation, sales managers usually focus on recruiting and selecting ("If we had more highly motivated salespeople to begin with, we wouldn't need such a clever compensation scheme"). So they have a brief romance with various testing and interviewing fads. Then they try training ("The salespeople don't know what we want or how to sell"). And finally they experiment with other motivational approaches like contests.

Although all of the foregoing are important, they should not be the only, or even the primary, consideration of sales managers. Sales management should be divided into two equally important parts: (1) formulating the sales policy and (2) implementing that policy. The first includes the detailed specification of the objectives, and the second, the accomplishment of the specified objectives.

Since the ultimate purpose of sales management is to generate loyal customers and high sales at reasonable costs, let us examine the four key questions that must be considered in formulating a customer-oriented sales program:

1. What is the general role that personal selling will play in the company's marketing strategy?

2. How will the salespeople be assigned or deployed to various customers and prospects, products, territories, and selling tasks?

3. How will each account and prospective account be managed?

4. What will the program cost, and will that cost be justified?

Role of Personal Selling

From management's point of view, the customer is served not only by the company's personal representatives but also by its total marketing strategy, including product policy, pricing decisions, distribution channels, and communications methods. Personal selling and advertising are the two primary methods of communication.

One of the major marketing decisions facing all companies, and particularly those marketing consumer goods, is that of personal selling "push" versus advertising "pull." The choice largely depends on the way in which consumers make up their minds, the influence different communications approaches have on them, and the relative cost of the different approaches.

On the one hand, advertising is inexpensive in terms of cost per person reached, but its impact is relatively low. In addition, the message is standardized, at least for each advertisement, and the flow of communication is totally one way. On the other hand, personal selling is expensive, but its impact is high. In addition, the message can be tailored to the individual customer, and the flow of communication is in both directions.

Often, companies forget that there are two intermediate points on the scale between media advertising and personal selling: *direct mail advertising,* which can be more targeted than media advertising but is still a one-way communication flow, and *telephone selling,* which is more expensive than direct mail but has greater impact, more flexibility, and is a two-way flow. Telephone selling is cheaper than face-to-face selling but has less impact. With the increasing cost of the face-to-face sales call (estimates now range from $60 to $70 for an industrial call), telephone selling has received new impetus. It eliminates travel time and expense.

Because of its expense, personal selling should be used only in situations in which (a) the high impact, flexibility, and two-way communication flow are needed, and (b) the high cost is justified. Personal selling can be most effectively used when it is carefully coordinated with other communications tools and other parts of the marketing strategy.

For example, a company may choose to deemphasize its personal selling effort and pass on the savings to the customer as a price cut. At the retail level, this has been part of the strategy of the discount store. Cash-and-carry wholesalers have also chosen this route.

Then again, some companies may choose to take over the role of their distribution channels and in the process to emphasize personal selling. Most consumer goods manufacturers have relatively small sales forces that call on wholesalers and retailers, who then sell the product to the consumer. Two major exceptions to this pattern are Avon Products and Fuller Brush, which employ large sales forces to sell their products directly to the consumer. To these companies, the personal selling effort is a basic part of their marketing strategy.

The customer is best served when the sales force is assigned only those tasks which it can perform more effectively and efficiently than other parts of the marketing strategy. Careful delineation of the role of personal selling in the marketing mix will help to prevent unfortunate situations in which sales managers attempt to motivate their salespeople to do things which are not in the interest of the company, the salesperson, or the customer.

Deploying the Sales Force

In assigning salespeople to territories, to accounts and prospective accounts, and to products, management should be aware that there are two parts to effective deployment: developing a policy and getting the salespeople to follow that policy. As we noted earlier, management sometimes emphasizes implementation of a particular policy without considering that it might have been incorrect to begin with. Let us return to the

Fitwell Company as an example of such a management error. Fitwell's mistake was at the policy level, in the deployment of the selling effort across accounts and prospects:

When sales of Fitwell's higher priced dress line failed to increase in spite of the product's known appeal, the sales management team decided to step back and take a fresh look at the entire selling effort. It soon became clear that the problem was one of deployment, not motivation.

The individual salesperson knew he or she could make more money by selling the traditional lower priced lines to existing customers than by prospecting for new accounts for the new line. To prospect effectively, the salesperson would have had to learn about a new product line, a new type of customer, and a new sales approach. Also, to the better salespeople who made in excess of $60,000 per year, the contests were irrelevant. They also knew that they were impervious to management displeasure as long as they were selling in the vicinity of $1,000,000 worth of merchandise per year.

It soon became obvious that these salespeople should never have been assigned to the new line. And once the problem was identified as one of deployment, the sales managers could cope with it. No longer did they harangue the sales force. Instead, they went about developing an additional new sales force that was recruited, selected, and trained to call on the new type of outlet. Field sales managers were given the responsibility of opening accounts that could use a sizable volume of the line.

In the end, everyone at Fitwell was satisfied. But everyone would also have been better off had the problem been carefully analyzed in the first place. If management had approached the situation properly, it would have seen that the choice was between having a new line with new retailers served by a new sales force or having no new line.

Deployment of the sales force across products, geography, and tasks (e.g., opening new accounts, selling, serving existing accounts) can be approached in the same analytical way (a) by striking a balance between policy development and policy implementation, and (b) by focusing on the generation and maintenance of profitable accounts.

Managing the Account

The development and maintenance of account relationships are especially important in business selling (e.g., one company selling to another) because in almost all instances the selling process is continuous—a supplier sells the same type of merchandise to a buyer over and over again. Since the market for most products is finite, each seller must constantly face the same buyers. This is less true for the consumer market, where there are many more buying units and where the repeat buying process is infrequent for many products, such as houses, television sets, and so forth.

ORGANIZATIONAL INTERACTION

An account must be defined in terms of both the organization and the individuals within it. Selling to an organization is much more complex than selling to an individual for two reasons: an organization is made up of different individuals with different needs, and those individuals interact with one another in complex ways. Consider the different explicit needs of the various participants in a purchase decision.

When a company buys a large piece of equipment, the manufacturing managers want an efficient machine that will require little repair and is technically advanced, the treasurer's department is interested in the financing terms, and the purchasing department is primarily interested in the total cost of the manufacturing system (e.g., raw materials, depreciation, installation) and the outright cost of the machine.

Consider also that the selling company must take into account the various participants' needs as well as their importance and power in the company. Every participant has both organizational needs, based on his or her position and professional interests, and personal needs. Buying decisions, because they involve authority and responsibility, represent a primary focus for the satisfaction of personal needs in the organizational setting.

Thus the young treasurer, say, might be trying to consolidate his newly won power by showing how well he can do the job. Then again, the manufacturing people might be smarting over a recent rebuff by the engineering people and therefore seeking revenge.

The astute company, sales manager, and salesperson should of course work hard to find out any information such as that just mentioned. Knowing the buying company's dynamics is part of what selling and account management are all about.

THE SELLING PROCESS

The actual sale consists of five sequential steps: opening the relationship, qualifying the prospect, presenting the message, closing the sale, and servicing the account.

The *opening* has the dual purpose of determining the right person in the organization to approach initially and of generating enough interest so that it is possible to obtain the information necessary for the qualification. The end result of a good opening should be an appointment with an appropriate and enthusiastic person.

The *qualification* is the process by which a salesperson determines whether or not the prospect is worth the effort of a sales presentation. Although scholars tend to gloss over the qualifying process, salespeople and sales managers constantly discuss it.

The *presentation* is the core of the selling process and requires astute management by the salesperson. It is the "pitch" (i.e., the actual attempt at persuasion). The presentation sooner or later culminates in an attempt to close the sale.

The *closing* is obtaining the final agreement to purchase. This is the Achilles' heel of many a would-be-successful salesperson.

After the sale comes the *service* aspect. Often the salesperson will be reselling supplies, materials, parts, and so on. This service part of the sale is frequently the opening to new sales.

Multilevel selling. Traditionally, the salesperson has sold to a purchasing agent in the industrial area or to a store buyer in the consumer goods field. Since it was a one-on-one relationship, the sales manager could structure his policies and programs on that basis. But the situation is changing, and the policies used to manage the sales force must now reflect these changes.

One important change is the introduction of multi-level selling—the process by which several authority levels are called on. The salesperson calling on a retailer, say, may attempt to contact both the buyer and the merchandise manager so that when the buyer seeks approval of the sales proposal, the merchandise manager is presold or at least receptive. Thus multi-level selling is in a sense a product of system selling because the chief buying influence (a) is at a higher organizational level than are the traditional buyers and (b) is responsible for the total system instead of just the individual components.

For example, consider the case of a manufacturing company for which one person purchases the raw materials and another buys the machinery. If the selling company wants to sell a system involving both raw materials and machinery, it is almost required to move upward in the purchasing organization to reach the chief buying influence in charge of both.

Team selling. The one-on-one selling process is further broken down by the introduction of team selling, a process in which several people from the selling company call on the buying organization. Thus, in a team approach, each level of the selling company calls on his or her counterpart in the prospective buying organization.

One reason for team selling is business etiquette (e.g., it is more appropriate for the national sales manager to call on the general merchandise manager than to climb beyond his or her own level or to descend beneath it). It also demonstrates appropriate interest on the part of the selling company's management. Still another reason is that this method allows for an exchange of power. The two top managers can make arrangements (e.g., private branding, special products) that their subordinates cannot.

Team selling is not limited to different hierarchical levels in the buying and selling organizations. Often it involves people in different functional areas in both companies. Members of different functional areas in the buying organization have specific needs and viewpoints that can best be met and understood by their functional equivalents in the selling organization.

For example, if the treasurer of the buying organization is concerned about financing arrangements, then the treasurer of the selling company is probably better suited to deal with that executive than is the salesperson, whose primary job is to deal with manufacturing and purchasing personnel.

There are three important considerations to keep in mind about team selling:

1. It is not always appropriate. Sometimes the sale is simple, repetitive, or small. The team approach is most suitable for the selling of heavy capital equipment or long-term supply relationships, either formal contracts or informal commitments. These involve enough dollars and enough different functions in the buying organization to justify team selling's high expenditure of time.

2. It is complex and difficult to manage. Actually, it is possible for the sales team to spend more time getting coordinated than selling. Or worse, it can spend too little time getting coordinated and end up presenting contradictory impressions to the buying influences.

3. It is in a sense an extension of the marketing concept that stresses the importance of having all parts of the selling company directed toward satisfying customer needs. Here, all relevant functional units become involved in the actual selling process.

Although team selling usually involves relatively high-level personnel and is used primarily to "open" an account, it can also involve lower level personnel and be used to provide continuing maintenance selling. A soft drink bottler, for example, may primarily use a route delivery person for selling but may supplement his efforts with an in-store display and merchandising expert. In other situations, inside sales liaison people, expediters, or shipping personnel may join the sales team in keeping accounts satisfied.

THE PYRRHIC SALE

The truly astute management is not interested in just making sales; it wants to build account relationships. These, of course, must result in sales sooner or later. The trade-off between immediate sales and long-term account relationships is part of the phenomenon that I call the Pyrrhic sale—one that immediately benefits the company but jeopardizes its future relationship with the account.

In business selling the customer is in the position of repeatedly being able to purchase the product. Thus this situation requires careful account management by the salesperson, who must be willing to forgo a sale that is not in the best long-term interest of the account and therefore of his relationship with it.

For example, the apparel salesperson who is willing to tell a customer that some items in his line do not sell well at retail in spite of their apparent appeal is helping his customer and himself over the long run. Or picture the response to the pump salesperson who says, "Yes, we offer the best pumps for your needs in applications a, b, and c, but unfortunately our pumps are not as good in application d as those offered by our competitors." The Pyrrhic sale, in contrast, occurs when the salesperson "forces" a marginal sale but risks losing the account.

THE SALESPERSON'S ROLE

Account relationships depend on more than just the salesperson's prudence in not pushing for orders. The salesperson can perform functions for the customer that make him or her valuable to the customer's organization. Two most important roles, merchandiser and ombudsman, are at the crux of the salesperson's account maintenance function.

As merchandiser, it is the salesperson's job to present those items in his product line which are most appropriate to the customer. In complex industrial situations, the salesperson is often responsible for designing the product to fit the customer's specific needs. In the apparel and furniture industries, the salesperson helps the buyer choose items which will sell best in his store.

As ombudsman, the salesperson is the customer's representative to the selling company in handling problems such as damaged merchandise, late or early shipments, credit arrangements, and the like. Obviously, the more effective the salesperson is in dealing with his own company, the more effective he can be in helping his customers.

THE COMPANY'S ROLE

The salesperson's function should not be the only important aspect of the company's account management procedures and policies. Many successful marketers develop special programs to help their customers. Some wholesalers, for example, offer site selection advice and store layout assistance to their retailers. Many companies provide their distributors with sales training assistance. Other companies help their dealers manage inventories.

Delivery and credit are two other important account management techniques. Fast delivery or emergency backup of spare parts inventories can cut down on the dealer's and user's inventory carrying costs. Special credit arrangements can help customers with their businesses. One important credit arrangement is "dating"— that is, extended credit provided in highly seasonal industries like toys that encourages the dealer to accept early delivery.

Some of these programs may be companywide, while others may be directed toward special categories of distributors or particular accounts. However, it is important to bear in mind that, according to the Robinson-Patman Act, all customers who compete with each other must be treated equitably.

As I indicated earlier, the nonselling parts of the company have an important role to play in account management. The rude receptionist and the truculent delivery man have probably lost as many accounts as the insensitive salesperson.

THE SALES MANAGER'S ROLE

All too often sales managers are more responsive to competitors than to customers in developing account management programs. Their attitude seems to be at best "we'll do it if they do it" but more often "it's a nice idea, but it costs money." They overlook the competitive benefits of being first with an innovative approach to customer satisfaction. They do not spend enough time thinking about the needs of the customer, because they are too busy motivating their salespeople.

Sales managers must make careful trade-offs between the costs of account management programs and the benefits to their customers. The ideal programs, of course, provide large benefits for small costs. Analytical, creative, and flexible sales managers can undoubtedly find a large number of approaches that meet this criterion.

The account management area is central to the difference between managing a sales program and a sales force. The real emphasis of the sales manager should be on customer management. The sales force should act as a conduit of communication, not as a barrier between the sales manager and the customer.

Understanding Selling Costs

In pursuing their ultimate objective of profitable account relationships, sales managers must look carefully at the cost of the sales force and the benefits received from it. Some of the concepts that we noted earlier in considering the role of personal selling in the marketing strategy are useful in deciding how much to spend on a sales force. The two primary determinants are the complexity of the selling task and the profit to be derived from the work done by one salesperson. The more complex the selling task, the more reason to have a talented sales force. The higher the profit created by a single salesperson, the greater the company's ability to pay for a "high-powered" sales force.

When the selling task is complex, the salesperson may actually be called on to "design the product" for the customer, as noted earlier. In tailoring the equipment to a particular customer's needs, the salesperson is developing a "product policy" for the smallest market segment— one buyer. To accomplish this difficult task, the salesperson operates in a customer-oriented, client-centered, problem-solving mode. He or she must transmit a great deal of complex intellectual information while providing reassurance in answer to psychological needs.

At the other extreme is the salesperson with the simple product whose function is to "go out and sell it." The mode is typically either persuasion or merely making the product available (e.g., the milkman). Little information needs to be transmitted. Often the task is merely to be "likeable," or at least not "unlikeable," and to actually deliver the products. Selling of this type demands only a low-powered sales force.

The high-powered sales force is expensive. The salesperson must be carefully selected. Often he or she has had substantial training prior to joining the company (e.g., the graduate engineer who sells complex equipment). Specialized training after joining the company is standard procedure. The only way to attract such an intelligent, trained, and trainable individual is to compensate well.

Usually, such a salesperson thrives on independence. A "programmed pitch" does not work. Geographical territories are often large, but the number of customers per sales person is small. Because each customer requires individualized service, the salesperson cannot cover many customers.

Other parts of the marketing mix also affect the nature of the selling effort. The more the company relies on sales service, the more it needs highly skilled salespeople. Conversely, if the company relies on its established reputation, innovative products, meticulous delivery, low price, or other attractions, the importance of the selling effort and the money available to pay for it are reduced.[1] The exhibit illustrates in diagrammatic fashion much of the preceding discussion on the nature of the selling task.

The Nature of the Selling Effort

		Simple	Moderately simple	Moderately complex	Complex
Aspects of the task	Mode	Persuasion or delivery			Problem solving
	Importance of information transmittal	Low			High
	Needs served	Personal and physical			Intellectual and psychological
	Where prevalent	Consumer and retail			Industrial and commercial
Profit impact		Low			High
Management of the sales force	Training	Less			More
	Compensation	Low			High
	Independence	Low			High
	Number of customers	High			Low
Typical examples	Consumer selling	Milk	Clothing	Real estate insurance	Stocks and bonds
	Industrial and commercial selling	Simple industrial supplies		Industrial equipment	High-volume OEM components
				Fashion at wholesale	Large private-label sales

Intricacy of sales task

VARIABLE VS. FIXED COSTS

The total amount is only one important aspect of costs; often the relationship of cost to volume is equally important. Media advertising costs are fixed; they do not vary with the unit sales volume. But sales costs may be either fixed or variable.

Sales overhead costs, such as the salaries of sales managers, are usually fixed. Sometimes, however, they include a bonus portion that varies with unit or dollar sales volume. Order processing costs are usually semivariable with the costs going up in a partially stepwise manner.

The major costs of the sales force itself may be either fixed or variable. A commission sales force, whether independent representatives or company salespeople, is a variable cost except for fixed salary guarantees, fringe benefits, and expenses. A salaried sales force is primarily a fixed cost. Usually, however, as sales volume per salesperson increases, there is a tendency to increase salaries.

The cost for a particular company of a straight-salaried sales force is directly related to the number of calls made. Clearly, if the number of calls a sales person can make in a given period of time is relatively fixed, the total number of calls which the sales force can make in a given period of time must depend on the number of salespeople. The number, in turn, is the key to the cost of the sales force.

Theoretically, expenses are a fixed cost. In practice, however, most companies are more liberal with expense money in times of high sales than in times of low sales. One could argue that this is contrary to the way it should be. When business is dismal, perhaps all possible action should be taken to increase expense money. Such reasoning is usually not followed, however, because the emphasis on cost control increases in poor times, especially among publicly held companies.

Sales promotion occupies an important point on the continuum between personal selling and media advertising. Some forms of promotion (like certain contests, presentation aids, and sales or distributor meetings) are fixed costs. However, price-off deals, special packages, certain other contests, and most types of promotions are purely variable costs.

Each type of cost has its own advantage. Variable costs are more conservative since they protect the company in times of poor sales (i.e., costs automatically decrease as volume does). Thus they lessen the effect of poor sales on profits. They also help those companies with a small share of the market.

On the one hand, whereas the largest competitor in a market can spread the fixed costs over the largest volume, yielding a low communication cost per unit sold, the smaller competitor does not have that advantage. If he spends as much per unit, his fixed costs of advertising or personal selling will be much smaller, but his program probably will not have as much impact. If the smaller competitor has as large a program, his costs per unit, and thus his percentage of sales spent on advertising or a salaried sales force, will be much higher, and his profits, all other things about equal, will be much lower.

On the other hand, competition on the basis of variable costs (like sales promotions) gives the smaller competitor a better chance. He can spend as much per unit as the larger competitor spends, yet enjoy equal impact.

Fixed costs have their advantages too. They offer great upside opportunity. As sales grow, costs increase more slowly and profits more rapidly. And as we just noted, fixed costs also provide the large competitor with an advantage over the smaller one.

Regardless of the situation, it is important for sales and marketing managers first to understand the relationship between costs and sales volume and then to build a program which provides the cost structure they desire.

Concluding Note

The customer ultimately determines the success (or failure) of a company's marketing approach. Every aspect of marketing, including the personal selling effort, must focus on the customer.

The sales force is important. It must be carefully managed. But in the final analysis, it is only a conduit to the customer. The object is customer satisfaction and sales. A disproportionate emphasis on the means must lead to a lack of attention to the objective. The prescription: manage the customer, not just the sales force.

Note

1. For evidence of the effect of company reputation on sales force compensation, see Richard C. Smyth, "Financial Incentives for Salesmen," HBR January–February 1968, p. 109.

Originally published in September–October 1974
Reprint 74512

About the Contributors

EDWARD C. BURSK was the editor of *Harvard Business Review* from 1947 to 1971.

THOMAS V. BONOMA was a professor of marketing at Harvard Business School, in Boston, and the founder of Renaissance Cosmetics, in Stamford, Connecticut. He authored several books and HBR articles.

KIMBERLY D. ELSBACH is a professor of management at the University of California, Davis.

HERBERT M. GREENBERG was the president and CEO of Caliper Management, a human resources consulting firm based in Princeton, New Jersey.

MARK KOVAC is a partner with Bain & Company in Dallas.

DIANE LEDINGHAM is a partner with Bain & Company in Boston.

HARVEY B. MACKAY is chairman of the board, chief executive officer, and sole owner of the Mackay Envelope Corporation, Minneapolis.

DAVID MAYER was a principal officer of Marketing Survey and Research Corporation of New York.

RONALD S. POSNER is the chairman of PS Capital, a firm that offers strategic and financial advice to companies. He is located in Tiburon, California.

BENSON P. SHAPIRO is the Malcolm P. McNair Professor of Marketing, Emeritus, at Harvard Business School in Boston. He is the author of numerous books and HBR articles.

HEIDI LOCKE SIMON is a partner with Bain & Company in San Francisco.

Index

Accenture, 14

account relationships. *See also* customer data; customer-oriented sales program; relationship development

account reviews and, 150–151, 162 (*see also* customer data)

company role in, 180–181

customer-oriented sales program and, 174–182

customer profiles and, 153–159

organizational aspects of, 174–175

personal touch and, 154, 155, 160

Pyrrhic sale and, 102, 179

sales manager's role in, 181–182

salesperson's role in, 180

selling process and, 175–179

senior sales force and, 98

separate divisions and, 118

special programs and, 180–181

strategic selling approach and, 101–102, 115–116

advantages, in major sales presentation, 120

advertising program

award-winning campaigns and, 31

customer-designed, 114

personal selling and, 65, 170–172

Adweek, 31

Aggreko North America, 10–11, 13, 16, 17

Allied Chemical, 99

artists, 24, 26, 31–33

AT&T, 125–126

attendees, and sales presentation, 111–112

attraction power, 134, 135, 137

authority, and power, 136, 138

automation, 13–14

automation, optimized, 13–14, 19–20

background blindness, 57–69

Bank of America, 104

Bell, 125, 140

buyer perceptions. *See also* pitchers, catcher's perceptions of

buying center approach and, 142–144

buyer perceptions (*continued*)
  schema for, 143
  stereotypes and, 23–40
buyers. *See also* buying decisions,
    analysis of; customer data;
    decision-making power
  buying urge and, 78–79, 84
  calculation of self-interest by,
    124
  as collaborators, 28, 30, 35,
    38–39, 74
  feeling of freedom and,
    67–69
  low-pressure techniques and,
    67–69
  top managers as, in major
    sales, 107–108, 111–112
buying-center concept, 129–133.
    See also multilevel selling;
    team selling
  behavioral clues to power and,
    138–139
  motivations of buyers and,
    139–142
  power bases and, 133–137
buying decisions, analysis of,
    123–147
  determination of buyer self-
    interest and, 124
  identification of decision
    makers and, 123–124,
    133–139
  organizational interactions
    and, 174–175
  psychological intelligence and,
    124
  roles in buying center and,
    129–133

buying urge, 78–79, 84

Campbell Soup, 152
Cantor, Nancy, 27
catchers. *See* buyers
champion power, 134, 137
"charity case" type, 40
Cisco Systems, 9–10, 13, 18
Citigroup, 12–13, 15, 18
Clausewitz, Karl von, 160
Clients for Life (Sobel), 21
closing the sale
  customer-oriented approach
    and, 176
  low-pressure techniques and,
    76–78, 85
  strategic selling and,
    114–115
Coca-Cola, 37
coercive power, 134, 135, 137
collaboration, with buyers, 28, 30,
    35, 38–39, 74
compensation plan
  incentives and, 16
  low-pressure selling and,
    91–92
  nature of selling effort and,
    184
  selling costs and, 185
conformity, and sales success,
    31–33, 52–53
Consumers' Research, 65
contract, in major sales presenta-
    tion, 121
contract sales, 99
conviction, 85–86
corporate jet buying process,
    126–128

cost justification
 in major sales presentation,
  120–121
 strategic sales and, 108–109
creative types, 24, 26. *See also*
  artists; neophytes; showrunners
creativity, and sales success,
  52–53
credit, and account management, 181
CRM software, 13
customer data. *See also* sales profile
 concerns about gathering, 147,
  156
 emphasis on, 147, 162–164
 gathering of, 124, 144–147
 human factors and,
  126–129
 personal information and,
  150–151, 153–159
 personal touch in sales and,
  150–151, 153–159
 productivity of sales calls and,
  144–146
 questionnaire form at Mackay
  and, 152–159
 sales force control forms and,
  146–147
 sources of, 154, 157–158,
  163–164
customer-oriented sales program, 167–187
 account management and,
  174–182
 role of personal selling and,
  170–172

sales force deployment and,
  172–174
 selling costs and, 182–187
customer-problem approach
 low-pressure selling and,
  63–64, 72–74, 83–84, 90
 risks in not using, 94–95
 selling costs and, 182–183
 threefold process in, 84–86
customer retention. *See* account
  relationships; human
  factors; relationship
  development

Dale Carnegie courses, 150, 161
deceit
 high-pressure selling and,
  66–67
 low-pressure selling and,
  70–72, 81–82
decider role, 130, 131–132
decision makers. *See* buyers
decision-making power, 123–147
 buyer motivations and,
  139–142
 buyer perceptions of sellers
  and, 142–144
 buying center concept and,
  129–133
 clues to identification and,
  138–139
 human factors and, 126–129
 identification of decision
  makers and, 123–124,
  138–139
decision-making power
 power bases and, 133–137
 team selling and, 177–179

Defying the Crowd: Cultivating Creativity in a Culture of Conformity (Sternberg and Lubart), 28, 36
delayed-action approach, 76–78. *See also* Number Two positioning
delivery, and account management, 181
deployment
    customer-oriented sales program and, 172–174
    scientific approach to, 16–18
deterrents to buying, and low-pressure selling, 79–80
"digital cockpit," 13
Dill, Mallorre, 31
direct mail advertising, 171
discounting, 125, 172
distribution channels, and personal selling, 172

economic conditions, and low-pressure selling, 87
ego drive, 41–42
    importance of, 47–48
    synergy with empathy, 48–50
emotional factors. *See also* customer data; human factors
    emotional appeals and, 69, 85
    low-pressure selling and, 69, 79–80
    resistance and, 79–84, 125–126
empathy, 41–42
    importance of, 46–47
    synergy with ego drive, 48–50
enthusiasm, 71

ethics, 70–72, 81
exaggeration, 70–71, 74
expense money, and selling costs, 185–186
experience
    background blindness and, 57–69
    inbreeding of mediocrity and, 55–57
expert power, 134–137

fakability, 51–52
field sales manager, 98
fixed costs, vs. variable selling costs, 185–187
frankness, 82. *See also* sincerity

gatekeeper role, 130, 131
GE Commercial Finance, 3, 5–9, 13
Gladwell, Malcolm, 29
goal setting, 9–11, 13, 14
Goizueta, Roberto, 37
gratification, and low-pressure selling, 78–79

"high and broad" calling, 107–108
high-pressure selling, 64, 66–67
Hollywood screenplay pitches, 25, 29–30, 32, 34–35, 36
human factors. *See also* customer data; emotional factors
    major purchasing decisions and, 126–129
    stereotyping and, 27–28
Humphrey, Hubert, 155

IBM, 14, 101, 125, 140, 152
implementation schedule, in
    major sales presentation,
    121
improvisation, 30–31
incentives. *See* compensation
    plan
indirect approach, 80–84
influencer role, 130, 131
initiator role, 129, 130
instant gratification syndrome,
    162
in-store support, 114
interest, and sales ability, 51
inventory management assis-
    tance, 180

Johnston, Wesley J., 133

Law of Large Numbers, 162
Leishman, Tim, 21
listening, 153, 161. *See also*
    customer data; customer-
    oriented sales program;
    empathy
location, and sales presentations,
    110
Lockheed, 99
low-pressure selling, 66–74
    customer-problem approach
        and, 63–64, 72–74, 83–84,
        182–183
    delayed-action approach and,
        76–78
    focus on objective and,
        84–86
    indirect approach and,
        80–84

letting the buyer decide and,
    67–69
reasons for effectiveness of,
    75–87
risks in approach, 92
sales force management and,
    88–93
selling effort in, 67–69
sincerity and, 70–72
special circumstances and,
    86–87
vs. high-pressure selling,
    66–67
Lubart, Todd, 28, 35

Mackay, Harvey, 150
Mackay Envelope Corporation,
    149–165. *See also* customer
    data
emphasis on salesmanship at,
    151–153, 165
"Mackay 66" device at,
    153–159
personal touch at, 154, 155,
    160
major sales. *See also* buying deci-
    sions, analysis of; strategic
    selling
buying center roles and,
    129–133
human factors in, 126–129
inclusion of top managers in,
    107–108, 111–112
low-pressure selling and,
    86
powerful buyers and, 133–139
risk and, 111–112
senior sales force and, 98

management processes, and
 sales support, 13–14
management summary, in major
 sales presentation, 120
McDermott, Bill, 4, 14, 15
McDermott, Lou and Sophie, 35
McMurry, Robert N., 43
mediocrity, inbreeding of,
 56–57
merchandiser role, 180
Mischel, Walter, 27
motivation
 for buying telecommunications system, 141
 diagnosis of, 139–141
 sales success and, 47, 48
 selling approaches and,
 141–142
multilevel selling, 176–177. *See
 also* buying-center concept

national account group, 117–118
neophytes, 24, 26, 34–36
nonselling time, 17–18
Number Two positioning,
 162–164. *See also* delayed-
 action approach

objective, focus on, 84–86
ombudsman role, 180
onetime sale
 opening and, 104
 relationships and, 102–103
 special sales force and,
 119–120
opening
 customer-oriented approach
 and, 175–176

strategic selling and, 103–104
 team selling and, 178–179
optimized automation, tools, and
 procedures, 13–14, 19–20
organizational factors
 account management and,
 174–175
 strategic selling and, 116–120

performance management. *See
 also* sales force; training
 customer profiles and, 157
 low-pressure selling and,
 91–93
 scientific approach and, 8–9,
 15–16, 20
personal selling, 170–172. *See
 also* low-pressure selling;
 top salespeople
personal touch, 154, 155, 160
"person prototypes," 27
Pilot, Michael, 3–5, 8–9
pitchers, catcher's perceptions
 of, 23–40
 artists and, 24, 26, 31–33, 37
 creative types and, 24, 26, 37
 neophytes and, 24, 26, 34–36,
 37
 risks in stereotyping and,
 36–38
 showrunners and, 24, 26,
 28–31, 37
 testing the pitcher and, 37–38
Popeil, Ron, 29
Porsche, 152
postsales service, 115–116, 176,
 183
power bases, 133–139

"practical intelligence," 28
procedures, optimized, 13–14,
    19–20
prospects
    qualification of, 104–105,
        176
    sales force deployment and,
        173–174
purchaser role, 130, 132–133
"pushover" type, 39
"Pyrrhic sale," 102, 179

qualification process, 104–105,
    176
question approach. *See also* col-
    laboration, with buyers
    low-pressure selling and, 74,
        83–84
    neophyte type and, 35
questionnaire form
    "Mackay 66" and, 153–159

rational buying
    benefits of buying and,
        140–142
    conviction and, 85–86
    low-pressure selling and,
        68–69, 79–80
    resistance and, 79–84
    trend toward, 65–66
recruitment
    aptitude testing and, 53
    high-powered sales force and,
        183
    for low-pressure selling,
        88–89
regional sales management, 98,
    117

relationship development. *See
    also* account relationships;
    customer data
    low-pressure selling and, 86,
        93
    personal touch and, 154, 155,
        160
    with top managers,
        107–108
    turnover and, 156–157
relationship sales consultants, 21
repetitive major sales
    consequences of, 99–100
resistance
    discounting and, 125
    low-pressure selling and,
        79–84 (*see also* emotional
        factors)
resource management, and
    strategic selling, 112–114
reward power, 134, 135, 137
Robinson-Patman Act, 113
"robot" type, 40

sales ability
    as fundamental to success,
        55–57
    other strengths and, 57–59
    sincerity and, 70–72
    training and, 60–61
sales aptitude tests
    central dynamisms and, 54–55
    reasons for failure of, 42,
        51–55
    use of empathy and ego drive
        in, 44–45
sales calls
    follow-up and, 160, 163

sales calls (*continued*)
  gathering data about buyers
    in, 144–146
  "high and broad" calling and,
    107–108
  initial contacts and, 159–160
  research before, 157–158
sales force. *See also* pitchers,
    catcher's perceptions of;
    sales force productivity; top
    salespeople
  costs and benefits of, 182–187
  deployment of, 16–18, 172–174
  makeup of, and major sales, 98
  nonselling time and, 17–18
  personal touch in training of,
    161–164
  recognition of salespeople and,
    165
  sales strategy and, 106–108
  third parties and, 104
  top executives as part of, 98,
    111–112, 118–119,
    159–160
  traits of salespeople and,
    24–26, 36, 54
sales force control forms
  psychological data and,
    146–147
sales force productivity
  four levers in, 1–2, 11–18,
    19–20
  optimized automation, tools,
    and procedure, 13–14,
    19–20
  performance management
    and, 8–9, 15–16, 20
  prediction of, 44–45

sales force deployment and,
    16–18
  size of force and, 6–7
  targeted offerings and, 11–13,
    19
sales forecasting, 9–10
sales leads, quality of, 104–105
sales manager, and customer
    benefits, 181–182
sales meetings, 91
sales presentation
  attendees at, 111–112
  elements in, 110, 120–121
  location of, 110
  order of, 110
  as step in selling process,
    109–112, 120–121, 176
  timing of, 111
sales profile. *See also* customer
    data
  evaluation of sales force and,
    157
  "Mackay 66" and, 153–159
  strategic selling and, 106–108,
    115
  type of information in,
    150–151
sales promotions, 186
sales reports, 91. *See also* cus-
    tomer data
sales training assistance,
    180
SAP Americas, 4, 14, 15
Savage Sisters sportswear line, 35
Schutz, Peter, 152
scientific approach to sales,
    1–21
  four levers in, 1–2, 11–18

at GE, 5–9
goal setting and, 9–11
productivity enhancement
and, 11–18
value of, 3–5, 18–19
scope, in major sales presentation, 120
"second sales force," 104
segmentation
deployment and, 16–17
scientific approach and, 5, 8,
16–17
targeted offerings and, 11–13,
19
"selection of facts," 70–71
selling costs, 182–187
nature of sales effort and,
182–184
variable vs. fixed costs and,
185–187
selling process, steps in, 175–176
senior sales force, 98, 117
service, as part of sale, 115–116,
176, 183
showrunners, 24, 26, 28–31
Sidhu, Inder, 10
sincerity, 63, 70–72, 82–83
site selection advice, 180
Smith Barney, 15–16
Sobel, Andrew, 21
solutions, in major sales presentation, 120–121
specialized knowledge, 86
special sales force, 117, 119–120
status power, 134, 136, 137
stereotypes
categories of creative types
and, 24–26

in human psychology, 27–28
negative, 27–28, 39–40
risks in reliance on, 26, 36–38
Sternberg, Robert, 27, 28, 36
Stone, Oliver, 24, 28
store layout assistance, 180
"Strategic Sales Opportunity Profile," 106–108, 115
strategic selling, 97–121
basic approach to, 100–103
buyer motivations and,
139–142
closing and, 114–115
cost justification and, 108–109
eight-step procedure for,
103–116
marketing as resource and,
113–114
opening and, 103–104
organizational techniques for,
116–120
perseverance and, 158, 162
presentation and, 109–112
prospect qualification and,
104–105
resource management and,
112–114
sales profile and, 106–108, 115
top executives and, 98
system selling, 99–100

talent retention
costs of turnover and, 42–43
scientific approach and,
15–16, 18–19
targeted offerings, 11–13, 19
team selling, 177–179. *See also*
buying-center concept

telecommunications systems,
motives for buying, 141
telephone selling, 171
territories
new, 77–78
restructuring of, 8
thinking, training for, 90
third parties, 104, 119–120
Thomson, Todd, 12–13, 15, 19
timing, and sales presentations,
111
Toastmasters course, 150, 161
top executives
buying center concept and,
131–132
first sales calls by, 159
human factors in selling to,
126–129
mental profile creation by,
155–156
relationship development and,
107–108
strategic selling by, 98,
111–112, 118–119, 159–160
TOPSales approach, 11–18,
19–20
top salespeople. *See also* talent
retention
ego drive and, 47–48
empathy and, 46–47
essential qualities of, 41,
46–48
failure of tests for, 50–55
fallacy of experience and,
55–59
as mentors, 20–21

permutations of empathy and
drive and, 49–50
role of training and, 59–61
senior sales force for major
accounts and, 98, 117
synergistic effects and, 48–50
training
fallacy of experience and,
55–57
low-pressure selling and,
89–90
mentors and, 19–20
nature of selling effort and,
184
nonrepetitive sales and,
119–120
personal touch in, 161–164
role of, 59–61
traits of salespeople
aptitude testing and, 54
creative behavior and, 36
creative types and, 24–26
turnover, costs of, 42–43

U.S. Equipment Financing, 3
"used-car salesman" type, 40
user role, 130, 132–133

variable costs, vs. fixed selling
costs, 185–187
veto power, 134, 137

Walker, George, 10–11, 17

Xerox, 140